Bible Words That Guide Me

*Seek ye out of the book
of the Lord, and read...*

ISAIAH 34:16

Bible Words That Guide Me

EDITED BY

HUBERT A. ELLIOTT

※※ ※※

PUBLISHERS

Grosset & Dunlap

NEW YORK

LIBRARY OF CONGRESS CATALOG CARD NUMBER: 63-12936

—»» «««—

*The contributors to this book
have graciously donated their royalties
from its sale to the
National Conference of Christians
and Jews.*

—»» «««—

Foreword

→→→ ←←←

The inspirational statements that make up this book were written by men and women of different faiths from all parts of the country.

They are clergymen, prelates, statesmen, teachers, actors, newsmen, businessmen, educators, artists, authors — in fact, a cross-section of America at its best.

They all share at least one thing in common — a dependence on a Higher Power, through the inspiration of Holy Scripture, to make their lives count and to be of service to their fellow men.

One of the many joys of compiling this book has been that of sharing the unassuming greatness of these contributors as they recreated from personal experience the effect on their lives of favorite Bible Words that have special meaning for them.

In this book will be found personal histories, stories of conflicts, philosophy, triumphs over adversity, and above all the strength of the Bible as a source of inspiration.

Here, in the great Judaeo-Christian tradition, are expressions of faith in God and in the dignity of man and his capacity for achievement.

HUBERT A. ELLIOTT

Contents

-»»-«««-

Bible Words That Guide Me

. . . aloha ke Akua.

JOHN 1:4-8 *Bingham Version*

DR. ABRAHAM AKAKA

Pastor Kawaiahao Church, Honolulu

AMONG THE FIRST WORDS taught by my father, Kahikina, and my mother, Annie, to all of their seven children were these: "Aloha ke akua" (God is love). Over the years, from infancy to adulthood, we learned many more verses from Ka Baibala Hemolele (The Holy Bible), but none meant more than or was used as often as "God is love."

"Aloha ke Akua" is associated first of all in my mind and

life with that place of quiet and peace when we gathered as a family to pray. Prayer-time is called Ohana in Hawaiian. Ohana literally means "Family" — a Family made up of father, mother, children, and God.

Every morning and evening of my life since earliest childhood, and even before I am told, my father and mother called their children to Ohana. In the morning about 5:45, there was a gentle touch of Pa's hand and the softly spoken words "Ohana kakou — Family prayer." We gathered in the living room in a circle, and Pa would lead in affirming of Scripture. Each of us would then say his favorite Bible verse in turn. "Aloha ke Akua" was never left out as someone's favorite verse in Ohana. We would not want to repeat any verse given by someone else, so the first one in the circle usually said "aloha ke Akua." After the whole family had joined as a choir in singing a hymn, Pa and Ma would lead in prayer — counting each blessing gratefully (even though we had very little in terms of this world's goods), remembering the needs of others, and asking God's guidance and care for the day.

Ohana added a dimension of deep understanding to the children as they grew — in terms of gratitude and love toward God and His love toward us and all people. Every evening, after dishes and homework were done, we gathered again in our circle to sing praises and thank God for the day and to pray for His keeping during the night. Not one day of the first 20 years of my life at home went by without Ohana morning and night.

Our family has stayed close to God and to one another all through the years. Ohana is kept by all my brothers and sisters and their families. By the love of God we are united, our lives are enriched and blessed in serving Him and our generation.

Secondly, in the history of Hawaii — the love of God is also manifest. The attainment of statehood for Hawaii is to me a culmination of the working of God's Aloha in Hawaii's life.

"Aloha ke Akua — God is love" looms large in my own life and in the life of Hawaii. May we help all mankind to experience the beauty and power of these words of St. John.

⫸⫷

ABRAHAM AKAKA is known by the affectionate title of "kahu," or shepherd in Honolulu and in all Hawaii. And many a visitor to Oahu's famed Waikiki Beach has been startled to discover after watching his expertise on a surfboard that "Abe," the powerfully built, brown-skinned Hawaiian, is not a beach boy, but a man who has been called the "best-loved minister in Hawaii."

Surfboard riding, of course, is a hobby. His vocation is people. As minister of Honlulu's Kawaiahao Church, the first built by the Congregational missionaries who reached Hawaii in 1820, as chaplain of the State Senate, and as a virtually indispensable man in almost every civic enterprise, Dr. Akaka normally works a 17-hour day seven days a week.

When Dr. Akaka took over the pulpit at Kawaiahao, which is known as "Hawaii's Westminster Abbey" (Hawaiian kings and queens were married, crowned, and buried there), he determined to make the church meaningful spiritually as well as historically. Reviving many ancient traditions, he can be seen standing in the pulpit in his stocking feet — a reminder that he who enters the church removes himself, to a degree, from the affairs of the world outside.

In this tradition-drenched church, the "kahu" makes many demands and imposes many disciplines on his flock. The church is nearly filled for daily ohana, or morning prayer service, which he instituted shortly after becoming minister of the church in 1956. Not only members of the congregation, but businessmen and government employes stop there to pray before they begin the day's work.

In addition to the discipline of daily prayer, Dr. Akaka requires his parishioners to tithe and serve the church. Not surprisingly, his congregation in turn adopted as its motto: "God first, others second, self last."

[5]

And He said unto them, Go ye into all the world, and preach the gospel to every creature.

MARK 16:15 *King James Version*

HARRY M. AYERS

Publisher, The Anniston (Ala.) Star

I OFTEN THINK of two versions of this verse in the Bible when I think of our fight against communism today. One of them is from Mark 16:15: "And He said unto them, Go ye into the all the world, and preach the gospel to every creature."

[7]

In Matthew 28:19, it is rendered "Go ye therefore, and teach all nations, baptizing them in the name of the Father, and of the Son, and of the Holy Ghost."

My father spent 25 years as a medical missionary in China, and I think it was the two quotations that I have given that had much to do with his making that sacrifice.

During his career, he was decorated by two Presidents of China and by several other persons in high places who believed in missions.

※※※

HARRY M. AYERS has been publisher of *The Anniston* (Alabama) *Star* since he acquired it more than a half-century ago. Through these busy years his philosophy has been: "The best way to build up a business is to build up the city in which the business is located."

Now past 75 years old, the publisher may be found daily at his desk at *The Star*. He purchased the old *Daily Hot Blast* in 1912, consolidating it with an afternoon paper to form *The Anniston Star*.

Since World War I, he has been a booster of the Army, which has given him many honors including the Ernie Pyle Award and the Outstanding Civilian Service Medal.

Education has long been one of his chief interests. He has been on the Alabama State Board of Education for more than 25 years and he holds honorary degrees from several colleges.

Also claiming the interest of the publisher for many years have been politics, veterans affairs, church endeavors, and business and industrial progress. He holds membership in several scientific and research groups and newspaper professional organizations. He was the first Alabama state chairman of the Crusade for Freedom, and he was the 1958 state Brotherhood Week chairman.

Colonel Ayers is a Sunday school teacher and a past president of the Anniston Rotary Club, which he helped to found.

Shadrach, Meschach, and Abednego
answered the king's threat of the fiery
furnace by saying:
*If it be so, our God whom we serve
is able to deliver us from the burning
fiery furnace...But if not,...
we will not serve thy gods.*
DANIEL 3:16-17

*Although the fig tree shall not blossom,
neither shall fruit be in the vines...
yet I will rejoice in the Lord.*
HABAKKUK 3:17

Though He slay me, yet will I trust in Him.
JOB 13:15

Jesus said: *Abba Father,...take away this
cup from me: nevertheless not
what I will.*
MARK 14:36 *King James Version*

DR. ROLAND H. BAINTON

Emeritus Titus Street Professor, Yale University

THESE VERSES might be called the "great nevertheless" passages, even though other expressions are used such as "yet" and "but if not." They all express a resolve to stand firm in the face of calamity.

[11]

Two of them have reference to conduct. The three Jewish youths would not falter even in case God did not deliver them from the fiery furnace. Jesus would not shrink even if God did not cause the cup to pass from him.

Two have reference to faith. The prophet Habbakuk would still rejoice in the Lord even though the land were despoiled by an invader, the crops ruined, and the cattle stolen. Job, even if his life were taken, would still believe in the goodness of God.

In our day there is so much to test faith and break down resolution that it is very heartening to discover others before us who were even more sorely tried and yet did not waver in their stand or in their faith.

-»»-«ᴇ-

ROLAND H. BAINTON is internationally known as a specialist in Reformation history and the life of Martin Luther. But he is a man of many facets.

He retired in 1962 after spending 42 years as a member of the faculty at Yale University where he made deep impressions on students and fellow faculty members.

Dr. Bainton has published 19 books, whose total sales are nearing 1,500,000 copies. And more books, he says, are coming. (His notable book, *Here I Stand,* the biography of Luther, and his church history for young people, *Church of Our Fathers,* were both best-sellers and have had several reprints.) He has preached and lectured widely.

He has been a caricaturist throughout his career—his sketches carrying sharpness and boldness. One of his mementos of a busy life is a book of these caricatures, going back many years, which includes sketches of Reinhold Niebuhr, Paul Tillich, Thomas Mann, Hendrick Van Loon, and scores of others.

Dr. Bainton, an ordained Congregational minister since 1927, continues to wield a deft pen both in scholarly work and in his works for students and laymen. A personal interest in the extension of Christian principles into everyday life is reflected in many articles and books.

A former student has described his mentor, Bainton, as "part puck, part Saint Francis, with a mixture of Erasmus gathered up in a mold provided for him by his English clergyman father."

Dr. Bainton joined the Yale faculty as an instructor in church history in 1920. When he became Titus Street Professor in 1936, which post he held until his retirement, he was its third incumbent in the century since it was established, in 1861.

Jesus wept.

JOHN 2: 35 *King James Version*

BRUCE BARTON

Honorary Chairman, Batten, Barton, Durstine & Osborne, Inc.

THIS is my favorite passage in the Bible because it says so much in so few words and shows that Jesus, even as you and I, had His problems.

BRUCE BARTON was born in Tennessee, the eldest of five children of the Rev. Dr. William E. Barton, an outstanding authority and author of books on Abraham Lincoln.

Bruce worked his way through Amherst College, selling aluminum cooking utensils from door to door during summer vacations. On his graduation, he took a job as time-keeper in a Montana construction camp. Six months later he returned to Chicago to become editor of a small religious paper and went on to a group of household magazines.

He came to New York as assistant sales manager with P. F. Collier & Son where with the encouragement of Mark Sullivan (at that time editor of *Collier's Weekly*) Bruce made his first appearance in print as a magazine writer. He became editor of *Every Week,* and subsequently was one of the most widely-published contributors to national magazines and newspaper syndicates.

In 1925 he published *The Man Nobody Knows* (Jesus), which was on the list of the six best sellers for almost two years, both in this country and in England. It has been translated into almost every foreign language and into Braille. *The Book Nobody Knows* (the Bible) joined its predecessor on the best seller list. His other books include *What Can a Man Believe* and *He Upset the World* (St. Paul).

While handling publicity for the United War Work Campaign, Mr. Barton met Roy Durstine and Alex Osborn with whom he formed a partnership, and in 1919 the advertising agency of BD&O opened for business. Before long it became one of the best known advertising agencies in the country. BDO merged with the George Batten Company in 1928 to become BBD&O. Mr. Barton is honorary chairman of the board.

In 1937 Mr. Barton was elected to Congress on the Republican ticket from the old 17th Congressional District of New York. He was elected by a substantial majority in a district more than two-to-one Democratic, and in 1938 he was re-elected to office. In 1949 as Republican candidate for the United States Senate he was defeated.

The famed writer and advertising expert gives freely of his time to humanitarian and civic causes and has served in national capacities for such organizations as the Institute for the Crippled and Disabled, American Heart Association, and the United Negro College Fund.

Behold, I have put my words in thy mouth.

JEREMIAH 1:1-10, esp. v-10b *King James Version*

DR. EUGENE C. BLAKE

*Stated Clerk, The United Presbyterian Church
in the United States of America*

IN A DAY when far too many religious persons seemingly prefer to remain silent on the critical issues that confront mankind, the experience of Jeremiah, as he heard the word of God, has a special significance.

The Scriptures bear witness to the fact that when God speaks to or through a man, the result is likely to be troubling, upsetting, exciting, awesome—most of all, disturbing.

So it was with the prophet. God spoke and His word broke through the routine of Jeremiah's formally religious life. To him there came the conviction that if he were really to do the will of God, he must speak out boldly and uncompromisingly on the religious, political, social, and economic problems that were facing the rulers and people of his nation. This proved to be neither a popular nor peaceful occupation.

As it was with the prophet, so it is with us. When God calls and we respond faithfully, we cannot help but be torn away from the peace and quiet of our religious existence and thrust into the excitement and pressures of the dramatic issues confronting our world.

The word that God puts in our mouths — the word he would have us speak for him — is a moral, spiritual, and hopeful word. He has called us, as he always calls men, to build and to plant as well as to root out and to destroy. He has called us to speak His disturbing and encouraging word.

Hear the word of God and live. Be certain that when God speaks, the ordinary, self-centered values of our culture that fall short of His will will be overthrown and we will be disturbed out of all complacency.

To my way of thinking, any religion that does less than that must be suspect on the face of it.

—»» «««—

EUGENE CARSON BLAKE, Stated Clerk of the three-million-member United Presbyterian Church in the U.S.A., is often considered to be a symbol of the unity many Protestant groups are seeking.

As chief executive officer since 1951 of the United Presbyterian Church (which as the name implies is itself a merger of two denominations), Dr. Blake speaks out frequently in support of church unity, racial equality, separation of church and state, and on other social and religious issues in the headlines of the sixties.

The burly six-footer and one-time Princeton football player is a man of strong personality, genial in conversation, and possessed of a wit that can be both sharp and droll.

In his role as an ecumenicist (he has held or holds high offices in both the World and National Councils of Churches), Dr. Blake proposed in 1960 and has since actively promoted the merger of all Presbyterians, Methodists, Episcopalians, and Church of Christ members in the United States into one new church. The potential membership of such a merger would be in excess of 18,225,000.

Dr. Blake, who has been called the nation's first statesman of Protestantism, has said he wanted to be a clergyman "ever since I can remember," and began preparing for this career as a youngster. After seminary graduation he held pastorates in New York and California before being named to his denomination's highest office.

The general public perhaps knows Dr. Blake best as master of ceremonies of the nationally-televised program, "Frontiers of Faith."

When not at his administrative office desk, he is filling the constant demand for his services as a speaker and as an ecclesiastical negotiator.

I will both lay me down in peace, and sleep: for thou, Lord, only makest me dwell in safety.

PSALMS 4:8 *King James Version*

DR. JOHN S. BONNELL

Minister Emeritus, Fifth Avenue Presbyterian Church,
New York City

IT WAS THE MORNING OF MAY 10, 1941. The sun shining in a cloudless sky lighted with unusual brilliance the whole expanse of La Guardia airport and its adjoining waters. The Pan American Clipper taxied out into the bay to a point from which it would make its starting run until it was airborne. In a moment the powerful engines roared into action and the Clipper cut through the waters like a knife. With incredible ease the bulky hydroplane

[23]

lifted itself into the air and at the height of a thousand feet began to circle the airport before heading out over the Atlantic.

Far below on the spectator's gallery I could see a blur of bright color where our three young daughters in their red coats stood beside our 16-year-old son and their mother. All of them were waving farewell. I frankly confess that while eager to get on with my mission of encouragement as a representative of the Protestant Churches in America to the churches of Great Britain, I nevertheless had some grave misgivings. It was no light matter to leave behind a wife and four children, the youngest of whom was but 10 years of age. With misty eyes I watched the little group until even the airport disappeared in the distance.

We headed toward spy-ridden Portugal. Our first stop for refueling was Bermuda, our second Lisbon, the "escape hatch" of Europe.

Little did we know that this night would be remembered in history for two separate occurrences: London was at this very moment undergoing the severest bombardment the city had suffered on any one occasion during the whole of World War II and Rudolf Hess was winging his way to Scotland.

As I watched through the porthole, the four propellers whirling in a halo of moonlight, a sudden fear smote me. How frail was the craft we were riding through the skies and how great was our dependence on these four motors! What would be the fate of my wife and four children if their bread-winner were suddenly taken away? My anxiety deepened with the passing minutes. It became almost unendurable.

Then suddenly into my mind a verse from the Psalms thrust itself. I could not remember at the moment in which of the Psalms it could be found nor when I had last read it. Nevertheless, every word became crystal clear to me — "I will both lay me down in peace, and sleep: for thou, Lord only makest me dwell in safety."

It was not that I regarded it in some sense as a guarantee of a safe voyage or of my sure return to America on the completion of my mission but rather as an assurance that both my dear ones and I myself were in God's keeping. I could trust Him absolutely for the outcome. In a moment of time the load of anxiety was lifted and my heart and mind were filled with peace.

⋙⋘

JOHN SUTHERLAND BONNELL, upon receiving an honorary degree from St. Dunstan's University in May, 1963, became the first Protestant minister ever to be honored publicly by that Roman Catholic institution in its 109-year history. He was awarded the degree in recognition of the service he had rendered in "the development of the dialogue between Roman Catholic and Protestant leadership."

Dr. Bonnell broke into a heavy schedule of speaking engagements to accept the accolade. Since his retirement in January of 1963 as Minister of New York City's Fifth Avenue Presbyterian Church, he has criss-crossed the United States dozens of times to conduct preaching missions and to create understanding among people.

This was the "retirement" the tall, distinguished clergyman sought when he stepped down from one of the most influential pulpits in the nation after 26 years in the same pastorate.

Long before he retired, Dr. Bonnell had been a tireless traveler. He had spoken in all parts of the world and had studied the social and religious conditions of almost all of Europe. In 1958, he led a five-man interfaith group on a goodwill tour of the Soviet Union, 15 countries in Europe, and the Middle East.

During his long pastorate at Fifth Avenue Presbyterian Church, Dr. Bonnell saw the congregation grow from 700 to 2,500 members. His parish duties for such a large church did not prevent him from being active in other causes for the good of the community and the nation.

He is a former President of The Protestant Council of the City of New York, the Protestant chairman of National Conference of Christians and Jews commission on religious organizations, the author of eight books, and a visiting seminary lecturer.

. . . whosoever will lose his life for my sake shall find it.

MATTHEW 16:25 *King James Version*

DR. LEE H. BRISTOL, JR.

President, Westminster Choir College

REMEMBER OUR LORD'S admonition against hoarding? He pointed up this lesson in His story of the man who buried his talent in the ground. This lesson, it seems to me, is aimed at revealing a kind of paradox: the fact that the more the Christian gives away his love and his faith, the more love and faith he himself will have.

[27]

If someone were to ask you to choose one Bible verse which you felt best represented the core of Jesus' teaching, what would you choose? Would you choose the Golden Rule, or a Beatitude, or maybe some verse from a parable?

My choice would be our Lord's words — quoted several times in the Gospels — about giving away one's life to find it, for those words seem to give us the central theme from which all other teachings flow. It might be said that of all the recorded words of Jesus these seem to be among the most profound.

An African native whom Dr. Albert Schweitzer had befriended stole from the great missionary, was caught, and later brought back, terrified, to face the doctor. "I am not angry," Schweitzer said, "only sad." A neighbor of ours whose young daughter had died of a brain tumor, went to console another mother who had just lost a child, and returned home stronger for what she had done. My own father was forever giving credit to others, it seemed to me, for what were often his own ideas. He did so, I suppose, because he believed in the greater good which could come from encouraging others instead of taking the bows himself. And a Christian civic leader told me after a successful city clean-up campaign, "When we forgot ourselves completely and thought about the good goals we had set for ourselves, it was astonishing how closed doors began opening for us."

The forgiving Schweitzer, the consoling mother, my father encouraging others, that civic leader learning the power of anonymity — all of these, unrelated as they seem, have in common the fact that they represent this emptying of self about which Jesus spoke when He said: ". . . whosoever will lose his life for My sake shall find it."

An anonymous poet once summed up this same theme in four lines:

"What! Giving again?" I ask in dismay.
"And must I keep giving and giving away?"
"Oh, no," said the angel, looking me through.
"Just keep giving till the Master stops giving to you."

LEE HASTINGS BRISTOL, JR., has excelled not only in the field of education but as a businessman, writer, composer, and civic and religious leader as well. As Edward R. Murrow once said in introducing him, these accomplishments are doubly remarkable in view of his age. He was born on April 9, 1923.

As an educator, Dr. Bristol is president of Westminster Choir College in Princeton, New Jersey; he is also president of the Creative Education Foundation. As a businessman, he guided Bristol-Meyers's public relations program until 1962, when he went to Westminster. A talented writer, Dr. Bristol is the author of *Seed for a Song,* the story of Bishop Robert Nelson Spencer. As a musician and composer, he has published many works in the choral and organ field. Although he specializes in sacred music and owns the desk at which his ancestor Thomas Hastings composed the familiar tune to "Rock of Ages," Dr. Bristol has also invaded the secular music field. In 1950, The *New York Times* credited him with writing the first piece of music played before the television cameras — a scherzo entitled "Laughter."

As a religious leader, Dr. Bristol is active in Protestant Episcopal Laymen's work and is a past president of the Laymen's Movement for a Christian World.

His philosophy, Dr. Bristol says, is that "a man's Sunday self and his weekday self are like two halves of a round-trip ticket: not good if detached."

Peace I leave with you, my peace I give unto you. Not as the world giveth, give I unto you. Let not your heart be troubled, neither let it be afraid.

JOHN 14:27 *King James Version*

E. W. BUCHANAN

Owner, Buchanan Service, Inc., Dover, Del.

SEVERAL YEARS AGO I became the owner of a stomach ulcer, which was diagnosed after many months of X-rays, examinations, and hospital visits. For a year or so I had suffered with intense stomach pains and nervous tensions from which I could not seem to get relief. Medication and strict diet did not seem to solve the problem as the pain and tension continued.

At one time I considered giving up my businesses that I had worked a lifetime to build up, in order to try to get rid of what I thought was bothering me. Finally I went to my minister.

I had always lived what I believed to be a Christian life but something was lacking. After many long conversations, he quoted the above verse of Scripture to me and raised the question as to whether or not I was taking Jesus at his word in my life.

Finally, after much prayer, I was able to accept the true meaning of this verse of scripture and what it could mean in my life. In my searching I also came across another verse which to me further implements the above promise: "And he arose and rebuked the wind, and said unto the sea, "Peace, be still! And the wind ceased, and there was a great calm." (Mark 4:39). When I could accept Jesus at his word, that he was leaving us his Peace, then a great calm came into my life. I still have all the problems I had before and more, but they don't bother me.

In times of business disappointments, reverses, loss of loved ones, and all the storms of life I have found that if I go to God in prayer and am willing to accept the promise that is expressed in my favorite verse of scripture, then that peace he is talking about comes into my life and there is a great calm that I never could experience before I found its full meaning.

→»» «««-

"BUCK" BUCHANAN loves and respects people. And people repay this trust by their confidence in the Dover, Delaware, businessman and civic and religious leader.

As the owner today of one of the nation's largest Firestone

tire distributor outlets, Mr. Buchanan has written of his earlier experiences: "As I look back on my beginning in business, I realize how other people have helped me to get going and have contributed largely to my success."

Similarly, people who have known him intimately or in a business way have paid tribute to his friendliness, to his honesty in dealings and actions, and to his deep principles based on Bible injunctions first learned from his mother as a boy.

It is these friends he has met and worked with over the years and "those who have helped him to be successful," as he puts it, that have given him his greatest satisfactions.

"The confidence so many hundreds of customers have shown in our Golden Rule method of doing business has been a very rewarding thing in my life," he says. "From the beginning I have operated the business by the Golden Rule, and that means a policy of being strictly honest with everyone."

Successful businessman that he is, Buck Buchanan is an admitted sentimentalist who has been known to help a boy short on cash arrange to buy a coveted bike, to help a struggling church in a depressed area make its witness known, to give deserving young men and women a lending hand on their way to college, and to bail out of jail some customer for almost any confinement except drunken driving.

*For if a man think himself to be something
when he is nothing, he deceiveth himself.
. . . no good thing will he withhold from
them that walk uprightly.*

GALATIANS 6:3; PSALMS 84:11 *King James Version*

ERWIN D. CANHAM

Editor, The Christian Science Monitor

MY MOST CHERISHED and useful Bible citation is two passages, read together. Years ago my mother, realizing the necessity of helping me to keep the ego in place, dinned into me the truth of:

> *For if a man think himself to be something when he is nothing, he deceiveth himself."* GALATIANS 6:3

As I was pondering this chastening reminder, she coupled with it from PSALMS 84:11.

"... no good thing will he withhold from them that walk uprightly."

Thus the lesson was complete: the freedom from a false sense of self, and the reward of impersonal good.

As I have thought this over, it has seemed to me very clear that St. Paul was telling us that material selfhood, flesh and blood, is the not the truth about man. Man's selfhood is spiritual. To "deny the flesh" is perhaps a great challenge. Nothing seems to me to be more important.

⁂

ERWIN D. CANHAM began newspaper work at the age of eight. While his father was country correspondent for a small Maine daily, Erwin would stand on a chair in front of a wall telephone, gathering village news from well-informed housewives of the neighborhood.

Later, when his father ran a small-town weekly, Erwin folded papers and then took an armful out on the street to sell.

From this printer's-ink background he progressed to reporter (at 14), proofreader, and galley-boy, a reverse of the customary order, because it was 1918-19, and the men on the small Maine daily were away at war. At Bates College he took part in many inter-collegiate debates, including the first held in the United States with a team from Oxford University.

He began work for *The Christian Science Monitor* as a reporter in 1925, took three years leave of absence as a Rhodes Scholar at Oxford, and worked between terms as a *Monitor* correspondent at League of Nations sessions in Geneva. He returned to the full-time staff and covered the 1930 London Naval Conference, served as Geneva correspondent, and was made chief of the paper's Washington bureau in 1932. In 1939 he was brought to Boston as general news editor, became managing editor in 1941, and editor in 1945.

Thus Mr. Canham's direct knowledge of the *Monitor* covers 38 of its 55 years.

One of the best-known American editors throughout the world, Mr. Canham is also active as a radio news commentator, television moderator, and public speaker. He is a dedicated public servant, having served in many official capacities with various national and international groups. Perhaps his most dramatic role as a humanitarian came when rebellious convicts in Boston's old Charlestown Prison asked for him as one of a group to enter a besieged cell block and help end a dangerous revolt. The dispatch he wrote after this experience is believed to have been carried on the front page of nearly every daily newspaper in the United States.

A man who has been described as one who works with both his head and his heart, Editor Canham has been called a practical idealist, a friend and adviser of many responsible public men, and an embodiment of *The Christian Science Monitor's* attitudes.

For unto you is born this day in the city of David a Saviour, which is Christ the Lord.   Luke 2:11 *King James Version*

GENERAL MARK W. CLARK

President of The Citadel,
The Military College of South Carolina

As I HAVE PROGRESSED from one phase of my life to another, different scriptural texts have appealed to me at various moments. At one point a certain scripture would serve best to comfort me and to give me resolution, whereas in another year a completely different text might fill the same need.

Last Christmas I was reawakened to the beauty of the Christmas story as found in Luke. My renewed interest in this portion of the Bible came about quite naturally. The Cadet Religious Council planned a Christmas program. for our students at The Citadel and their guests. Featured in this spiritual emphasis program were the cadet voices of The Citadel Choir and the Glee Club from a local girls' school. I was asked to read the scripture.

On the night of our service we were amazed to find that our huge, beautiful chapel was packed with people. There was a complex traffic jam on our campus, and people were crowding the entrances to the chapel in an effort to hear the music. We had reserved areas in which the choir could sit when not singing, but the press of the crowd became so great that we permitted guests to take these areas and the members of the choir agreed to remain standing throughout the program.

As I heard my voice take the beautiful message of the Christmas story out to this great, eager congregation, the scripture took a new hold on me. The full impact of Luke's writing was felt when I read "For unto you is born this day in the city of David a Saviour, which is Christ the Lord."

Because of this incident, and the fact that I received a tremendous "lift" from this scripture at a time when my spirits were low, I can say that today it is my favorite text, while knowing that tomorrow in another situation a new text may come to mean just as much in my life.

⇛⇚

MARK W. CLARK, who was Supreme Commander of the United Nations in the Far East, culminated a soldier's career in two world wars by bringing about an armistice in Korea.

But he did not consider the truce either a victory or a defeat. He called the achievement the most "frustrating, tedious, and disheartening task" that had been given him in his 40 years in uniform. And he used the occasion when New York City later honored him with a traditional ticker-tape parade to warn the nation against dropping its guard against the "treacherous Communists."

The tall, ramrod-straight West Pointer had dealt with the Red Army in Austria, with Russian diplomats in Moscow, and with Chinese and North Korean Communist leaders in Panmunjom.

General Clark served in the Far East until 1953 when he formally retired from the Army and accepted the presidency of The Citadel, The Military College of South Carolina, in Charleston, where he assumed office in 1954.

During his Far East assignments and in' World War II, those who came into contact with the General describe him as being a soldier who never appeared to worry and one whose manner was "totally unruffled." He had the reputation of being a democratic and kindly officer but one, when the occasion called for it, who could be "rock-firm and unyielding."

General Clark, who was wounded in World War I, was the leader of a thrill-packed secret mission by submarine to North Africa just before the 1942 invasion there. The mission was successful — but his group barely escaped capture and he, himself, was thrown into the sea when a small boat capsized.

After the North Africa victory, General Clark commanded the major forces in the Italian campaign, and his Fifth Army captured Rome; the first enemy capital to fall to the Allies. The Fifth was the first American Army to be activated in the European theater and it saw some of the hardest fighting of the war. The General won many decorations for his leadership.

President Truman in 1951 appointed General Clark, an Episcopalian, to be the first full-fledged U. S. Ambassador to the Vatican. The appointment was later withdrawn, at Clark's request, ending a storm of protest from groups opposed to the appointment.

Behold, I stand at the door, and knock: if any man hear my voice, and open the door, I will come in to him, and will sup with him, and he with me.

REVELATION 3:20 *King James Version*

GEORGE CORNELL

Associated Press Religion Editor

OVER A LIFETIME, a certain number of doors are going to be slammed in your face. Sometimes it comes as a shock. Always it hurts. And sometimes it is shattering. Nevertheless, that is the way of the world. Inevitably doors will be closed against you.

Moreover, our whole civilization is plagued by "closed doors," by barriers between nations, between races, between cultures. We have a hard time getting through to one another. We are shut off, enclosed, thwarted. The walls and the doors barricade us from our goals, and from each other.

A person can learn to live steadily with this fact, so long as he knows that while some doors may close, others still are open, and are to be found. That is the conviction that keeps us engaged and devoted to life.

Only if the impression develops that all the avenues are blocked, that further effort is useless and that every alternative is a dead end, only then do we lose touch with that magnificent sustainer, hope. Of course, at times, we all hit bottom. We have those moments when it is hard to recognize the still unlocked doors.

Often it is a matter of job prospects that don't materialize, of plans that don't go through, of love that finds no response, of interference, sickness or unforeseen demands that deter us and hem us in. We can't avoid these obstacles, these closed doors. They are part of our environment.

Yet, to me, the regenerating fact is that the one basic door, the underlying gateway of all our lesser bypaths and doors, is always accessible. Not only does it open to us, but it proclaims a constant invitation.

The assurance is summed up in that strangely beseeching passage in Revelation 3:20: "Behold, I stand at the door, and knock: if any man hear my voice, and open the door, I will come in to him, and will sup with him, and he with me."

This is a marvelous truth to me, and an amazing reinforcement. The one door that counts in this sometimes frustrating journey through time is never bolted, never shut against us. It beckons us, calls us to swing it wide, and breathe deep of the refreshing currents flowing through it.

Of course, we need to keep banging away at the rigid and wretched little doors that beset our families, our neighborhoods, the places where we work, and our world. But at the same time, we gain the footing and the balance for that by affirming, and laying hold on that one door, so sensitive to our touch.

Personally, this old verse from the apocalypse of St. John

had a lot to do with focusing my life, and bringing me to a clearer realization of just where the main threshhold lies, and of its predominant importance in relation to all the rest of the subsidiary doors. Consequently the verse will always have a particular preciousness to me.

Oddly enough, too, that preeminent door has a way of working on all the other doors, making them seem less formidable, less defeating. They are there, yet to be licked, but they can't lick you, when the main route is clear.

I've noticed that in several places, scripture uses the image of a door to picture God's entry among us. "I am the door," Jesus is quoted in John 10:7. And again, in Revelation 3:8, he says: "Behold, I have set before you an open door, which no one is able to shut . . ."

The trouble with us is that we so often fail to use it. It is there, close by. And the rapping at that door never ceases, deep within the human consciousness. We can keep ourselves preoccupied with our trivial, stubborn little back-doors, side lanes and basement windows, and fold up in moans because we so often can't seem to budge them. Yet, towering about them all, the main gate is always open. We have only to let down the bars of self to give access for abundance in our empty rooms.

-》》》 《《《-

GEORGE W. CORNELL, one of the nation's outstanding writers on religion has been a member of The Associated Press staff since 1947.

As a specialist in the reporting of religious news, George W. Cornell's byline is known by readers throughout the country, particularly through his perceptive weekly column for morning papers, "Religion Today," which is widely printed.

The AP staffer has reported most of the major world religious news events that have taken place since World War I, in which he served as an Infantry Lieutenant. The Associated Press has carried to its member-papers news reports filed by Cornell from Rome's Second Vatican Council, New Delhi's World Council of Churches Assembly, and from wherever in this country the great gatherings of religious bodies are held.

[45]

Blessed are the merciful for they shall obtain mercy.

MATTHEW 5:7 *Challoner-Rheims Version*

RICHARD CARDINAL CUSHING

Archbishop of Boston

THERE ARE SEVEN WORKS of spiritual mercy and seven works of corporal mercy. These works of mercy must be accompanied by three conditions to render them perfect and acceptable to God.

I must extend them to all without exception, even to my enemies. I must take advantage of every occasion of doing good, in every type of distress, and exert myself to the utmost of my ability. I must accompany them with interior motives and interior devotion. A good intention can sanctify an action which might otherwise be only good.

Christ is the perfect example of this beatitude. He addressed all mankind when in His mercy He said, "Come to me, all you who labor and are burdened and I will give you rest." He took advantage of every occasion for doing good. He taught daily in the temple. He went about doing good and healing all who appealed to Him. He performed these works of mercy with the most tender affection, for He acted like the good Samaritan, who bound up the wounds of him who fell among robbers. Therefore, I must go and do also in like manner.

The reward attached to works of mercy is great. If I perform them I shall obtain mercy. This mercy will accompany me in this life. It will extend to both body and soul. It will be my reward in the next life — with what measure I measure, it shall be measured to me. I stand in need of God's mercy, and miserable would I be if God dealt with me according to my deserts.

I must be merciful to others that I may obtain mercy. "Judgment is without mercy," writes St. James, "to him who has not shown mercy."

⟫⟪

RICHARD CARDINAL CUSHING has a keen appreciation of the spiritual needs not only of his flock that numbers more than 1,500,000 but of the entire world.

Few church leaders are held in such warm esteem as is the lean, good-humored, self-denying Archbishop of Boston.

When Pope Pius XII named him Archbishop in ˙1944, Cushing was then the youngest man of that rank in the Roman

Catholic hierarchy. He immediately launched a greatly-needed renovation and construction program in his archdiocese. Altogether, he has spent more than $50,000,000 on schools, hospitals, and other institutions and millions of dollars more on churches, chapels, and charitable services — all of which, under his policy, were debt-free when placed in service.

His high spirituality and physical vigor are known and admired by people of all faiths from all walks of life. His work for more than 20 years for the missions of the Church has made his name known throughout the world wherever there is a Roman Catholic mission.

The Cardinal's magnificent power of oratory has been coupled with clear, direct, and powerful pronouncements that cover a wide range of subjects, from pastoral matters to his views on the "problems of society." He has written cogently on the personal relationships of Roman Catholics with others in a pluralistic society, the breakdown of moral behavior, and the growing ecumenical spirit of "Catholics, Protestants, and others."

Nowhere is his powerful leadership more apparent than from the pulpit and the rostrum. He appears frequently on local and national network television. The Cardinal's day begins at 6 a.m.; he keeps two corps of secretaries busy from 8 a.m. until after 10 p.m. Yet he somehow finds time to make himself available to all who wish to consult with him.

When the Archbishop received his "red hat" in 1958 (on being declared a Cardinal by Pope John XXIII), he was already recognized in the United States as one of the nation's pre-eminent religious leaders.

The affection that people hold for him everywhere is perhaps summed up best by a rabbi who lives near the Cardinal. The rabbi said Cushing was "a revered prince of the church who has gained love and respect of myriads of fellow citizens of every religious denomination and racial ancestry. Our community is blessed by his presence."

The land that was desolate and impassable shall be glad, and the wilderness shall rejoice, and shall flourish like the lily.

And the redeemed of the Lord shall return, and shall come into Sion with praise, and everlasting joy shall be upon their heads: they shall obtain joy and gladness, and sorrow and mourning shall flee away.

ISAIAH 35:1 ... 10* *Douay Version*

*Only the first and last verses are shown here, since the entire passage cannot be encompassed on the page.

MRS. AGNES DOOLEY

Author

My FAVORITE PASSAGE is to be found in Isaiah, and consists of all ten verses of Chapter 35. It is my favorite for the simple reason that it contains — in the profoundest sense — good news, movingly and beautifully expressed.

While its basic message is one of joy and optimism, it also takes note of the sorrows and tragedies of life. The references to illness and human frailties in this passage always remind me of a letter which my son, Dr. Thomas A. Dooley, sent me from the shrine of Our Lady of Lourdes. He wrote this letter during his first visit to France, when he was only 21 and still in medical school:

> "My trip to Lourdes was a strange one. It has an odd fascination; I was shocked, but I loved it too. It's rather difficult to explain. To see so much sheer hopelessness, so much dreadful deformity, such weeping . . . I did have a sort of peaceful feeling while looking up, but was torn apart when looking around me."*

This sense of the duality of our existence is perfectly reflected in these verses, whose message is one of courage, strength and refreshment in the face of desolation, weakness and sorrow. In the final verse comes the wonderful news — the promise of redemption and everlasting joy. These are indeed Bible words to live by.

-»»-«««-

AGNES DOOLEY is the mother of Dr. Tom Dooley who grew up in the heart of America — and won the heart of the world.

Mrs. Dooley, twice a widow, still lives in the Dooley family home in St. Louis where Tom was born.

In her first book, *Promises to Keep,* published in 1962, Mrs. Dooley tells about her son who became a national legend for his compassion, generosity, dedication, and supreme courage.

He was a typical American boy in an average family — yet he became one of the heroes of our time as a Naval Doctor

---

* From PROMISES TO KEEP, copyright © 1962 by Agnes W. Dooley and Malcolm W. Dooley, and used by permission of the publishers, Farrar, Straus and Cudahy, Inc.

treating nearly half-a-million natives in Vietnam, as organizer of *Medico* to provide medical care for people in areas of the world where no care was available, and as a builder of hospitals in Laos. Dr. Dooley, who was called "the splendid American," became a victim himself — of cancer, from which he died in 1961.

His mother's book is a reverent and beautiful memorial to her doctor-son whose practice included all humanity.

I am the light of the world; he that followeth me shall not walk in darkness, but shall have the light of life.

JOHN 8:12 *King James Version*

LADY MALCOLM
DOUGLAS-HAMILTON

THE GOSPEL OF ST. JOHN is so filled to brimming with glorious promises by Christ to men and women who love and believe in Him, that it is hard to choose one single passage over another. Other Gospels may speak of compassion or humility or charity, but St. John deals with the great shining power of the risen and eternal Christ himself. He establishes a direct, unbreakable power-line between the glory of God and the frailest human life. For me, in times of stress, tragedy or decision it has opened great wellsprings of strength and confidence.

Who could not fail to find the "faith that can move mountains" when we hear Christ saying to us those thrilling words "In this world ye shall have tribulation, but be of good cheer, I have overcome the world." Set-backs, misunderstandings, disappointments, heartbreaking problems all seem to fall into a different perspective and the hurt miraculously removed when we say these words. Christ is telling us that He has already won for us whatever battle we are fighting.

Some people feel that St. John's Gospel is too mystical and do not quite understand it. But what could possibly be more direct and to the point than what he says to us — "I am the Resurrection and the Life. He that believeth in me, though he were dead, yet shall he live." This Gospel tells us in words of one syllable that each of us is an integral part of Christ — that we are His and He is ours. "Whosoever believeth in Him should not perish but have everlasting life."

Time and time again all through my own life, I have sought solace and refreshment and received strength from these words. Whether it be pacing the hospital floor praying for a loved one in childbirth or waiting by the long hours to hear from my husband on a dangerous flight, I repeat over and over the words, "Whatsoever ye shall ask in my name, that will I do." And I know that God's will will be done, and reviving waves of comfort sweep over me.

It is difficult for me to learn how to stop working at an appointed task soon enough and I often arrive suddenly at the far end of my strength and near complete exhaustion. I now stop completely and remember what Christ said, "I am come that they might have life and that they might have it more abundantly." I then try to relax completely and allow that very abundant, life-giving force of Christ to enter in.

Many people, over the years, have asked me, "where do you get your energy?" and "why are you always so happy?" It is very simple. I just ask God continually to guide and strengthen me, and show me what to do — that His will be done — not mine. And I read again the inspiring words of St. John and remember that Christ said, "I am the light of the world; he that followeth Me shall not walk in darkness, but shall have the light of life."

-》》《《-

LADY MALCOLM DOUGLAS-HAMILTON is widely known as the leader and founder of organizations and movements to uphold American ideals, strengthen its freedom-loving allies, and combat international communism.

In 1939 she founded and was the president of Bundles for Britain, famous American war relief agency for the British people and armed forces, which had 2,000 branches in the United States, two million volunteer workers, and sent many millions of dollars worth of clothing, surgical equipment, and supplies overseas.

She subsequently formed Bundles for America and Bundles for Bluejackets for the American armed forces.

After six years as special assistant to the publisher of *The New York Times,* she resigned to found the pioneer anti-communism organization, Common Cause. It served as the original contact between the American people and the exiled Eastern European leaders as well as many underground movements. The organization sponsored the famous Old Berlin Rally, obtained the writ of habeas corpus for Mrs. Oksana Kasenkina when she leaped from the Russian Embassy, and organized the original Freedom Rally.

Boston-born Lady Douglas-Hamilton has played a leading role in many civic, educational, and religious organizations. She holds an honorary Doctorate of Humanities degree. She is a member-at-large of the Board of The Protestant Council of the City of New York and a Commander of the British Empire.

[57]

*And other sheep I have, which are not of
this fold: them also I must bring,
and they shall hear my voice; and there
shall be one fold, and one shepherd.*

JOHN 10:16 *King James Version*

GEORGE DUGAN

New York Times Religion Editor

MAN HAS SOUGHT for centuries to mend the broken strands of Christendom. Progress has sometimes moved with glacial slowness, if at all. Theologians have quarreled with other theologians and the layman's confusion has been compounded. Selfish man has himself set up obstacles that bear no relation to Christian love.

Yet Christ's desire for "one fold, and one shepherd" cannot be submerged.

Signs of hope are everywhere. Leaders of a tragically divided Christianity are now examining areas of agreement — not differences. There will be many discouragements, much misunderstanding.

But in our time leaders of Protestantism have broken bread with prelates of Rome and patriarchs of Orthodoxy have found common cause in ecumenicity.

Fertile ground is being plowed in high places by the Second Vatican Ecumenical Council and the World Council of Churches.

A new breed of theologians is in our midst. They are the "ecumenists," pioneers in Christian unity who have raised their cause from avant garde to summit priority.

Jesus Christ, one hopes, could never have foreseen the bitter rivalry within His church. But his words in the Gospel of John are prophetic for today: "and there shall be one fold and one shepherd."

-》》-《《-

GEORGE DUGAN, Religion News Editor for *The New York Times,* has covered most major religious events during the past thirteen years in this country and many of those abroad, including all three assemblies of the World Council of Churches (Amsterdam, Evanston and New Delhi) and the Second Vatican Council in Rome.

He started his career in religious journalism shortly after he graduated from the University of Michigan. He has been with *The Times* since 1949. Mr. Dugan has talked with clergymen of all faiths in covering religious news. As a result, he has made Page One of *The Times* with many by-line accounts of religious activities. He believes, as does his paper, that religion is full of important, increasingly significant news for everyone.

Mr. Dugan has been an on-the-spot observer at the great contemporary church gatherings where the unity of Christendom is being sought. The knowledge and understanding of Christian, Jewish and other religious concepts reflected in his objective reporting have won him many citations, including an award of merit from the National Religious Publicity Council for his "outstanding service to religion."

⫸ ⫸ ⫸ ⫸ ⫸ ⫸ ⫸ ⫸ ⫸ ⫸ ⫷ ⫷ ⫷ ⫷ ⫷ ⫷ ⫷ ⫷ ⫷ ⫷

But now abideth faith, hope, love, these three;
and the greatest of these is love.

I Corinthians 13:13, *American Standard Version*

ADMIRAL E. M. ELLER

Rear Admiral, USN (Ret.), Director, Naval History Division

ONE WHO LIVES THIS LIFE thoughtfully realizes early or late that a hand mighty and blessed, but firm, directs all his hours. In some mystic way we have free rein, yet we are always steered on a general course "preordained before the world was born."

In part it is like a ship of sail that tacks on one course,

[63]

then another far different to keep the wind, then another still — yet always trends towards a chosen port for which she never steers directly until the last moment.

I say in part, because the captain of a ship knows where he steers and that each leg has a vector that makes toward the goal; whereas in life each of us is blind against the future. However when we look backward at the wake whence our course has run (if we look with faith and acceptance) we see that it has always made toward a definite purpose for good. Even the darkest disappointments and despairs at last reveal themselves as necessities that have led to the *summum bonum* of one's life.

This knowledge comes slowly, and groping humans that we are, must be relearned often — fortunately less often as one voyages on beyond mid-passage. Hence one's favorite Bible passage changes with the years. As a young man I preferred most of all, "Ask and it shall be given you, seek and ye shall find, knock and it shall be opened . . ."

I still believe firmly in this passage and its companion "Have faith in God. Whosoever shall say unto this mountain . . . and shall not doubt in his heart . . ." I believe even though I have often been given just the opposite of what I asked — an opposite that has proved better than I could conceive.

However, after years as a man, out of loved passages in this book of the soul that should be our first care in education, play and vocation, a preferred group took shape for me from separate books: "This commandment which I command you this day is not hidden from you, neither is it far off . . . but it is very nigh unto you that you may do it . . .

"Thou shalt love the Lord thy God with all thy heart, and with all thy soul . . . This is the great and first commandment and the second is like unto it, Thou shalt love thy neighbor as thyself . . .

"And now abideth faith, hope, love, these three; and the greatest of these is love."

Surely if one abides by these he will find bearing him up "the everlasting arms." Surely in greatest trial he can say,

"The Lord is my light and salvation, whom shall I fear."
Surely he will follow the star, "Seek ye first the kingdom
of God and his righteousness . . ."

The kingdom of God is love. If one directs all his courses
with love as the star, and has faith that God guides where
he steers, and has hope for "the everlasting arms," then he
steers a true course into eternity.

→→→ ←←←

ERNEST McNEILL ELLER, known to his friends as "Judge,"
is Director of Naval History. This scholarly sailor early showed
parallel bents in history, writing, and science. Born in Virginia and brought up in North Carolina, he taught high school
mathematics and history before entering the United States
Naval Academy. There he wrote extensively and founded the
literary magazine of the midshipmen.

After graduation he served in submarines, aircraft carriers,
and battleships and established the Fleet Anti-aircraft Machine
Gun School afloat.

On shore duties, "Judge" Eller taught at the Naval Academy.
The range of subjects included leadership, history, English,
and ordnance and gunnery. In those years he wrote a number
of professional, technical, and historical articles and books.

In 1940-41, he served in the British Fleet and experimental
stations, observing anti-aircraft and other war developments.
On his return to the States, he helped develop close-range anti-
aircraft weapons and fire control and initiated anti-aircraft
training centers ashore before joining the *USS Saratoga* as Gunnery Officer in 1941.

Just before the Battle of Midway he reported to Admiral
Nimitz's staff for gunnery, fleet training, and preparation of
battle analyses and action reports. In this capacity he participated in several amphibious operations including Guadalcanal
and Okinawa and in the last months of the War commanded
assault transports.

Since 1945, Admiral Eller has served as Head of the Navy's
Public Information Bureau, on the Staff of the Joint Chiefs
of Staff where he participated in setting up the military side
of NATO, as Commander of the Middle East Force and, after
retirement, as Director of Engineering at Bucknell University
before being ordered back to active duty as Naval Historian.

*If thou hast run with the footmen, and they
have wearied thee, then how canst thou
contend with horses? and if in the land
of peace, wherein thou trustedst, they
wearied thee, then how wilt thou do
in the swelling of Jordan?*

JEREMIAH 12:5 *King James Version*

DR. BERGEN EVANS

Northwestern University Dept. of English, Evanston, Ill.

OUT OF THE GREAT TIDES of sonorous and passionate rhetoric that make up the Bible, I would not want to pick up any single verse as pre-eminent, but the above Jeremiah 12:5 — has always had a deep personal meaning for me.

In an hour of despair in my young manhood I told a great aunt of mine who had brought me up as if she were my own mother that I could not go on, that crushed under sickness and poverty, I wanted to give up all the plans that she and I had made for my education. Just as I was leaving she spoke this verse to me and, it so happened, these were the last words I ever heard her speak.

They have stayed with me as a sort of tribute to her and to her indomitable spirit that met despair not with soothing but with increased and sterner challenge. And they have served, in their dignity and mournful beauty, to help me to understand — now that "many pastors have destroyed my vineyard" — the sway that the Bible exercised over minds such as hers.

Our village was drab and commonplace, its industries were grimy, its shops poor and bare, its pleasures few and dreary. Yet under the witchery of this great Hebrew poetry it was to her, apparently, a place where foot soldiers strove and horsemen contended in battle and where, but a little beyond, the rising waters of an awful and mysterious river offered in an exciting and glorious challenge access to God.

⇒⇒⇒ ⇐⇐⇐

BERGEN EVANS is a learned teacher, author, and radio and television personality who commands the respect of students, scholars, and the public-at-large.

As a professor of English at Northwestern University, his classes are noted for the stimulation they engender among his students and the effect his published work have on the campus in general and throughout the educational community.

Scholars respect Dr. Evans for his learned contributions as an author and as a writer for professional and other publications. He has written several important books, including *A Dictionary of Contemporary American Usage.*

And he is well known as the witty, erudite moderator of the radio and television program, "The Last Word."

In addition to his professorial and platform renown and the popularity of his books, Dr. Evans is widely respected as a discerning book reviewer.

And as ye would that men should do to you,
do ye also to them likewise.

LUKE 6:31 *King James Version*

HARVEY S. FIRESTONE, JR.

Chairman, The Firestone Tire & Rubber Company

ONE OF MY favorite passages from the Bible is from St. Luke 6:31, "And as ye would that men should do to you, do ye also to them likewise," which, down through the ages, has become known as the Golden Rule.

These fifteen words are the key to our hope for world

peace and brotherhood of man. They set forth clearly and concisely the way of life that an all-wise Creator intended us to follow.

I believe that the application of the Golden Rule, the use of prayer and the practice of brotherhood, constitute the keystone of true Christian living.

A man has only one life. He cannot divide it up into a business life, a church life, and a social life. Therefore, he should try to apply his Christian precepts in his office, in his home, and wherever else he meets with his fellow man.

And to me, this can be done by remembering the words in St. Luke's Gospel and by applying the Golden Rule to every decision that touches upon the rights of others and our own responsibilities to humanity.

-》》 《《-

HARVEY S. FIRESTONE is the active head and chief executive of a world-wide industrial organization that is in the select ranks of companies doing over a billion dollars worth of business a year. The Firestone Tire & Rubber Company is one of this country's 34 largest companies and was voted one of the 10 best managed by a special panel of 171 corporation presidents whose findings were published in *Dun's Review*.

In the course of a distinguished career, Mr. Firestone has been named one of the 12 outstanding businessmen of the United States in a survey conducted by a leading business magazine.

Despite heavy business responsibilities, he has nevertheless for years given generously of his time to worthwhile civic, religious, educational, and humanitarian activities. Part of this country's economic and cultural progress stems from the sense of duty and personal responsibility found in men such as Harvey Firestone and the Firestone family.

In the tradition of his distinguished father, who was one of America's great industrial and civic leaders, Mr. Firestone is serving numerous causes for the welfare and prosperity of the United States and for peace throughout the world.

*To every thing there is a season, and a time
  to every purpose under the heaven:*
*A time to be born, and a time to die; a time
  to plant, and a time to pluck up that
  which is planted;*
*A time to kill, and a time to heal; a time to
  break down, and a time to build up;*
*A time to weep, and a time to laugh; a time
  to mourn, and a time to dance;*
*A time to cast away stones, and a time to
  gather stones together; a time to
  embrace, and a time to refrain from
  embracing;*
*A time to get and a time to lose; a time to
  keep, and a time to cast away;*
*A time to rend, and a time to sew; a time to
  keep silence, and a time to speak;*
*A time to love, and a time to hate; a time
  of war, and a time of peace.*

ECCLESIASTES 3:1-8 *King James Version*

*If I take the wings of the morning, and
  dwell in the uttermost parts of the sea;*
*Even there shall thy hand lead me, and thy
  right hand shall hold me.*

PSALMS 139:9-10 *King James Version*

COLONEL JOHN H. GLENN, JR.

Lt. Colonel, USMC, Mercury Astronaut

"EACH INDIVIDUAL is innately blessed with certain talents and capabilities, but it is up to each of us to determine how we are going to use these talents and capabilities. To a great extent, within the above limits, our lives are what we make them." This was the thesis of some of my early parental teaching. The more experiences I have had, the more I am convinced that this is true.

The first quote indicates to me that we are not only permitted, but expected, to live life to its fullest — to make the most of every talent we have. We will not always be right. We will make mistakes, but at least we keep trying. According to this scripture, there is a time for everything, a time for use and exercise of all our talents, and it is our privilege and responsibility to determine the "right season for every purpose."

The second quote tells us that no matter where we take these talents — no matter what we try to do, whether it's good or bad, right or wrong, in or out of season — we will never be alone.

›››‹‹‹

COL. JOHN H. GLENN, JR., the first American astronaut to orbit the earth, gave the Senate Space Committee a simple outline of his religious faith a week after his historic feat.

The Lieutenant Colonel in the U.S. Marine Corps stated that he could not say he sat there and prayed while he was in orbit. "I was pretty busy," Colonel Glenn said. "In the past, people have tried to put words in my mouth on this."

The 40-year-old Mercury Astronaut was interrupted by applause when he added that he felt a man should live his life as though every day might be his last. He said he personally falls so far short of this goal that it is "pitiful," but he will always come back and try again.

"My religion is not of the fire-engine type — not one to be called on only in an emergency for a 24-hour period and then put God back in the woodwork," Colonel Glenn told the Senate Committee.

"I am trying to live as best I can. My peace has been made with my Maker for a number of years, so I had no particular worries on that line."

I hate, I despise your feasts,
And I will take no delight in your
    solemn assemblies.
Yea, though ye offer me burnt-offerings
    and your meal-offerings,
I will not accept them;

Neither will I regard the peace-offerings
    of your fat beasts.
Take thou away from Me the noise of
    thy songs;
And let Me not hear the melody of
    thy psalteries.
But let justice well up as waters,
And Righteousness as a mighty stream.

                — AMOS 5:21 *Masoretic Text*

HARRY GOLDEN

Editor, The Carolina Israelite

AMOS WAS A SHEPHERD, a working man, and his prophecy was the first — or so I have always read it — with a social protest. It is the basis for the great rationale of the sanctity of the individual. Amos argues that God is not interested in the forms of ritual the people may invent, but in their idealism, in their ability to see other men as men and not as simply shepherds or kings, or Samaritans, or Hittites, or Gentiles, or Ethiopians. Amos prophecizes that each individual is important, each is the be-all and end-all of His work.

God does not care whether people stand or sit or kneel when they worship, or whether they mass choirs to sing His praise, or build tall buildings to His glory. God wants justice, and He wants the people to want justice. We know from the philosophers that justice comes to us only when the man who is *not* injured anguishes and feels as much pain as the man who *is* injured.

Centuries later, Immanuel Kant wrote that the Categorical Imperative consisted of treating every man as an end and never as a means. Amos said it first, and in the mighty rhythms with which he surrounded it he forever thrills me with both pride and resolution.

→》》 《《←

HARRY GOLDEN has been called one of the last representatives of personal journalism in this country.

Through his Charlotte, N. C., weekly, the *Carolina Israelite,* his best-selling books, his syndicated newspaper column, and his frequent television appearances, Mr. Golden probably enjoys as large a following as any writer in America.

But Harry Golden considers himself first and foremost a newspaperman.

In October of 1962, after Mr. Golden had completed 20 years of his unique journalism, he told a Chapel Hill, North Carolina, audience that he felt he had fulfilled his function as a newspaperman "because first I'm a newspaperman, a newspaperman before I'm a Jew, an American, a Zionist, and a Democrat."

Mr. Golden founded his own personal journal, the *Carolina Israelite* in 1944 with a subscription list of about 400. The circulation increased steadily and then skyrocketed to more than 35,000 following publication of his book, *Only in America* which became a best-seller.

As a personal journalist, Mr. Golden considers "a memory that sometimes frightens me" and "an uninterrupted record of reading books" as the assets necessary for his chosen field. His wit and philosophy — expressed both in his writings and in his public appearances — have made him the best-known editor of a weekly paper in America.

⇶⇶⇶⇶⇶⇶⇶⇶⇶⇶⇶⇶⇇⇇⇇⇇⇇⇇⇇⇇⇇⇇⇇⇇

*Being confident of this very thing, that he
which hath begun a good work in
you will perform it until the day
of Jesus Christ.*

PHILIPPIANS 1:6 *King James Version*

DR. BILLY GRAHAM

Evangelist

I HAVE AUTOGRAPHED thousands of Bibles, and the text
that I always write my signature below is Philippians 1:6:
"Being confident of this very thing, that he which hath be-
gun a good work in you will perform it until the day of
Jesus Christ." To me, this verse in Paul's letter to the
Philippians garners the finest of Biblical truth, both in the

Old and New Testaments, and concentrates it in capsule form which is easy to grasp.

This verse struck me forcibly when as a young man I wrestled with some doubts and misgivings about God and His revelation to man. My faith was of a wavering variety, and I came to the place where I was in no position to help others while I myself was so faltering. This greatly disturbed me.

One day, at a retreat for young people, I went out into the woods to meditate and pray. I made up my mind that on that day I would either give up what little Christian faith I had or discover a stronger base upon which to stand for Christ. I opened the Bible, and this verse caught my attention: "He which hath begun a good work in you will perform it until the day of Jesus Christ." It dawned upon me that what faith I had was a gift of God, that His reserves were boundless, that if I would consent to receive, He was ready, willing, and able to keep on giving. From that day to this He has never stopped giving and performing that which He has begun.

I inscribe this verse in the Bibles of new converts because it delineates so clearly the steps of living for Christ.

"Being confident" — Faith is the launching pad that projects the believer into his eternal orbit. I watched the astronauts climb into the nosecone of their giant rockets, aglow with confidence. After dozens of tests, they were confident that all would go well and "A-OK" was the watchword. For centuries tests of faith have been going on, and God has never let a man down yet who had confidence in Him, and He is not going to begin with you!

"That He" — Christian faith reposes not in a ritual, a creed, a system but in a person, Jesus Christ. His name when mentioned in history invokes reverence. The world's great have paid Him homage, but He is more than a figure of history; He is the living, redeeming, forgiving Lord, the same yesterday and today and forever.

Then the last phrase of the verse ".... until the day

of Jesus Christ." The Christian is a refugee, an alien in this world, but someday he will come into his own, in the day of Jesus Christ. This world rightfully and legally belong to Jesus Christ. It is His by right of creation, and it is His because He redeemed it by His blood. The Bible teaches that someday ". . . . the kingdoms of this world shall become the kingdoms of the Lord and of His Christ."

In this verse we see the importance of personal faith, "being confident of this very thing", the progressiveness of God's power in our lives: "That he which hath begun a good work in you will perform it," and the ultimate triumph of righteousness ". . . . until the day of Jesus Christ." Here is a bulwark against the fears and frustrations of these times. Here is a pathway to peace in a warring world. Here is a source of strength when many are wavering before the challenges of the 1960s. Here is confidence, resolution and hope!

-»» «««-

BILLY GRAHAM has become an American institution. He heads a remarkable organization that has prepared the way for him to go literally into all the world preaching the gospel.

A native of North Carolina, Dr. Graham was called to the ministry in 1934 at the age of 16. Since then, he has preached to millions, both in person and over the world's radio and television networks. It has been said that he has probably been seen and heard by more people than any other religious leader in history.

Billy Graham has become the friend and counselor of Presidents, Kings and Queens, Prime Ministers, Church prelates— and of the people.

Dr. Graham's famed Crusades have been one of the religious phenomena of this century; they have resulted in inspiring thousands of people, whom he describes as "hungry," to hear the story of redemption—to accept morally and spiritually a new way of life as Christians.

Behold, how good and how pleasant it is for brethren to dwell together in unity.

PSALMS 133:1

. . . and they shall beat their swords into plowshares, and their spears into pruninghooks: nation shall not lift sword against nation, neither shall they learn war any more.

ISAIAH 2:4

. . . and what doth the Lord require of thee, but to do justly, and to love mercy, and to walk humbly with thy God?

MICAH 6:8

But Jesus said, Suffer little children, and forbid them not, to come unto me: for of such is the kingdom of heaven.

MATTHEW 19:14

And ye shall know the truth, and the truth shall make you free.

JOHN 8:32

Pure Religion and undefiled before God and the Father is this, To visit the fatherless and the widows in their afflictions, and to keep himself unspotted from the world.

JAMES 1:27 *King James Version*

DR. FRANK P. GRAHAM

United Nations Representative for India and Pakistan

THE BIBLE needs no word of mine to add to its own story, long told in personal lives and in human history. These frail words are not by way of addition but by way of simple acknowledgment.

The Bible, in various parts and ways, is one of the foundations of three of the world's great religions: Judaism, Christianity, and Islam. For thousands of years, the Bible has been for hundreds of millions of "People of the Book" the source of faith and humility, strength, and hope. The Bible is the progressive revelation of God in the life and experiences of a great people and the life and meaning of Jesus.

First in the Bible were the highest conceptions of one God, the moral law, and the potential meaning of sacrificial love in human affairs. Influential in life and history have been the Bible's Ten Commandments, the continuing struggles of human frailty for personal goodness, the unresting aspirations of imperfect human society for the prophetic social justice of a free society, the Sermon on the Mount, the Lord's Prayer, the life, teachings, joys, and sufferings of Jesus as the Son of man and Son of God.

Some passages in the Bible have precious meaning for me in the added emphasis on them in their own lives by the dearest and two of the noblest people I have known: my mother, who was the mother of nine and a whole neighborhood of children; and my wife, who was the mother of a University community of students. In their minds and spirit the neighborhood and the community came to include the world.

These favorite passages include those above and also the Twenty-Third Psalm, and I Corinthians 13:1-13.

Powerful in life and history are these facts: Jesus preached the gospel to the poor; ministered to the sick and hungry; redeemed the fallen with forgiveness; chose as an example of brotherhood a member of a despised people; taught "man cannot live by bread alone"; "the Sabbath was made for man, not man for the Sabbath"; "I and the Father are one and ye are my brethren"; associated with publicans and sinners; made merry at the wedding feast; drove the money changers from the temple; set his face steadfast to take the Jerusalem road; said,

"Father, forgive them for they know not what they do"; suffered, died, and triumphed over death with spiritual power for the sacred dignity, equal freedom and abundant opportunity of all persons, now and hereafter, as the children of one God and brothers of all people on the earth as the home of the family of man.

-»» «««-

FRANK P. GRAHAM — "Dr. Frank" as he was addressed by students when he was President of the University of North Carolina — is a man small of stature and frail in appearance. But he has been described as a "giant."

Through his distinguished service to his native Tar Heel State, the United States, and the United Nations he has come to be considered a champion of the rights and the dignity of the individual.

At Chapel Hill, where he was a professor from 1914 to 1939 (with time out for Marine Corps duty in World War I) and University President until 1949, Dr. Graham was noted for his patience and his abilities as a teacher. An able public speaker, he was as much in demand at student pep rallies as he was on various public platforms. But his real forte is his talent for working with small groups to bring people together.

A lovable man, who in turn loves people, Dr. Graham as University President — and later as a United States Senator — was often in the center of controversy as he fought for what he called the rights of the minority. He was on the alert at Chapel Hill to thwart any move to restrict academic freedom. And he put his many talents at the service of various causes in which he believed, ranging from equal suffrage for Negroes to federal aid to the states for public schools.

Dr. Graham's integrity and independence have been praised and are respected even by those who do not accept his views.

His abilities were recognized by President Roosevelt who used Dr. Graham's talents in a number of appointive positions, including membership on the War Labor Board. After the war, he served as a U.N. mediator in the Dutch-Indonesian clash. Since 1951 he has been a United Nations mediator for India and Pakistan.

[89]

*Truly, I say to you, as you did it to one of
the least of these my brethren,
you did it to me.*

MATTHEW 25:40. *Revised Standard Version*

DR. GEORGIA HARKNESS

Professor Emeritus of Applied Theology
Pacific School of Religion, Berkeley, California

THESE WORDS MEAN MUCH TO ME because they epitomize
the Christian obligation to reach out in sympathy and compassion to serve one's fellowman, and to do so in the spirit
of brotherhood at the call of the Father of us all.

In common with our Jewish friends, we of the Christian
faith believe that God is the Creator and Ruler of all the

earth, and that He has made all men in His own spiritual image. He has placed us here to love one another and to be responsible stewards of the good things of life which He has placed so bountifully in the earth. Nevertheless, both men and nations more fortunately situated than others have acquired material goods and the facilities for health, education, and human welfare far beyond what others enjoy and are inclined to regard them as their own. As a result two-thirds of the world's population are underfed while we overeat and — to say nothing of adequate medical and educational facilities — millions lack adequate clothing and shelter to protect them from the elements.

The injunction to Christian compassion and service is a direct obligation stemming from the two great commandments to love God supremely and to love our neighbor as ourselves. It is everywhere manifest in the life and ministry of Jesus, and it comes to startling vividness in the parable of the great last Judgment in which the words quoted above appear. Our place in the kingdom of God, not at the end of time, only, but at all times, depends on our caring enough in outgoing concern to feed the hungry, clothe the naked, minister to the sick, and welcome the stranger in Christ's name.

I cannot say exactly when in my own experience this conviction came home to me. Perhaps it began as a child in my simple rural home when we sat down to a meal and my father would thank God for it and my mother would say as she so often did, "I wish everybody had as good." In my college days I felt deeply the impulse to missionary service in foreign lands, though circumstances have never permitted me to become a missionary in the usual sense. In my adult years of teaching religion in college and seminary I have naturally had occasion to interpret many aspects of the Christian gospel, including both theology and the devotional life; yet I have always tried to put them in the context of the call of God through Christ to serve the brother in need. This obligation came home to me with great vividness a few years ago when I taught and traveled in the Orient, and especially when I saw in Hong Kong the plight of many thousands of refugees from Communist tyranny.

Service to the brother in need is, of course, not the only aspect of the Christian religion. Whether as clergy or laity, we must reverently worship God both in church and in our private devotions; we must seek to discover what God says to us through the Bible, and endeavor both to acquire and to transmit our great Christian heritage; we must establish Christian homes; we must be the Church within the world, making our Christianity relevant to many aspects of business, community and political life.

Indeed, personal compassion is not enough. We shall not solve our economic racial and political problems until it has been translated into great social structures. Nevertheless, the first step is to feel a deep Christian concern for all persons, created and beloved by God, Christ's brethren and ours. The primary imperative toward a better world for all mankind is to take seriously the words, "Truly, I say to you, as you did it to one of the least of these my brethren, you did it to me."

⟫⟫⟫⟨⟨⟨

GEORGIA HARKNESS began dreaming of becoming a missionary as a girl in rural New York.

When family considerations prevented her from going into this field, she taught school for several years. Later she attended Boston University to take courses in philosophy and theology. She has described this latter experience as something that really challenged her enthusiasm for the first time.

She was ordained in 1926 as a minister of the Methodist Church — and during the busy, productive years since then, Dr. Harkness has been challenging the best in people.

Through her teaching (she is Professor Emeritus of Applied Theology at the Pacific School of Religion in Berkeley, California); through her books (24 have been published), poems, and hymns; and through her participation in numerous ecumenical gatherings Dr. Harkness has become one of Protestantism's most influential leaders.

"With men it is impossible, but not with God: for with God all things are possible."

MARK 10:27b *King James Version*

DR. LAURENCE D. HASKEW

Vice Chancellor, The University of Texas System

WHO IS IN CHARGE HERE?

The first time I remember really seeing the text quoted above was on a little hand-lettered card on the desk of Dr. George Washington Carver at Tuskegee Institute. I was about 14 at the time. Through several ensuing years of close friendship between Dr. Carver and my father, a Methodist minister, I saw it again many, many times — in the life attitude of this great man.

One instance stands out particularly. Dr. Carver drove down to visit my father one day. Dad did his best to get him to get out of his car and come in the house, to no avail. We all knew why. Dad grew a little bitter in his comments about the hopelessness of changing blind social customs which affronted human dignity and, incidentally, punished ministers for practicing brotherhood. Dr. Carver smiled and said, "Dan, God is in charge here, too. With Him all things are possible. The important word is *with*."

I misunderstood that message for a long, long time. I thought it said that if I and other men would just ally ourselves with God, success would bless our efforts. The road to alliance was a tough one, but eventually we could get God on our side. My approach was sincere, my efforts reasonably arduous and many miraculous things occurred. But I never did make the grade, and neither did the principalities and powers that seem to control the destiny of mankind on this little solar satellite. Individually and collectively it was apparent that we were camels engaged in futile endeavor to get through the eye of a needle. We could not even think what salvation meant, much less achieve it.

My dilemma was fairly obvious. I could believe that no One was in charge here, really. It is a finite system — this business of being alive. Our Creator gave us biological equipment, environmental forces, some leeway to make what we and He at least call free choices and then withdrew to watch with interest His cosmic experiment. The past makes the present and the present makes the future, and stupid mortals make all three. Salvation is impossible and hence does not really exist; the only realities are an inchoate individual soul and a chaotic corporate mind which can and do blow millions of us to hell constantly and at any moment can make the job complete. With men, *this* is possible and anything else is impossible.

The alternate horn of the dilemma is another kind of God. Dr. Carver's kind. William Penn's kind. St. Francis' kind. Martin Buber's kind. Mary Magdalene's kind. Jesus Christ's kind. He *is* in charge here. With Him, all things are possible. He wants and yearns for my salvation. Only dimly can I discern what He is up to, but I can grasp His objective — that rich men, intellectual men, confused men, depraved men, mistaken men, and just plain stupid men realize that the impossible has already happened; the eye of the needle has become the Eye of God. With confidence and out-welling love, I can take my place behind my piled-high desk — a place in an infinite system with God in charge both here and there — trying my best to let God do my little bit in that system.

To choose this latter way of life was and is impossible for me. That it *is* chosen makes me realize what Dr. Carver was testifying with his radiant life-phrase, "With Him all things are possible."

⇒⇒⇒ ⇐⇐⇐

LAURENCE D. HASKEW joined the University of Texas faculty in 1947 as College of Education dean. He became a vice chancellor of the University System in 1954.

He asked to be relieved of the deanship in 1962, after giving leadership for 15 years to the College of Education and public education throughout Texas. He continues to serve as a professor of educational administration in addition to his administrative duties.

Dr. Haskew is active in Austin, Texas, community activity and religious life, and he travels extensively as a speaker and consultant. He has held several national offices, including the presidency of the American Association of Colleges for Teacher Education and membership on the Educational Policies Commission of the U.S. His book, *This Is Teaching,* has been recognized as one of the outstanding publications in its field.

Before going to the University of Texas, Dr. Haskew had been a director of teacher education at Emory University and at Agnes Scott College, and a public school superintendent, athletic coach, and high school principal in various Georgia cities.

He has taught at the University of Georgia, Georgia Teachers College, Columbia University Teachers College, New York University, and Stanford University.

[97]

*Blessed are the poor in spirit: for their's is
the kingdom of heaven.*

*Blessed are they that mourn: for they shall
be comforted.*

*Blessed are the meek: for they shall inherit
the earth.*

*Blessed are they which do hunger and thirst
after righteousness: for they shall
be filled.*

*Blessed are the merciful: for they shall
obtain mercy.*

*Blessed are the pure in heart: for they
shall see God.*

*Blessed are the peacemakers: for they shall
be called the children of God.*

*Blessed are they which are persecuted for
righteousness' sake: for their's is the
kingdom of heaven.*

MATTHEW 5 : 3 - 10 *King James Version*

BROOKS HAYS

Special Assistant to the President of the United States

IT WOULD BE IMPOSSIBLE for me to designate one verse or
chapter as my favorite. Matthew 5 (with the Beatitudes
and the immortal sayings of Jesus) is one favorite. And the
matchless Thirteenth Chapter of I Corinthians is another.
But there are other passages that I like to recall, and the

choice would probably depend upon my mood and my need.

I recall, for example, in some of the crises of my political life the help derived from the Psalms. Terrific pressures sometimes pile up for the politician. In sleeplessness I have repeated to myself certain lines which indicate that Scripture is designed to help men in harassment and difficulty.

The author of the lines ". . . Oh that I had wings like a dove! for then would I fly away, and be at rest." (Psalms 55:6) reflected a feeling we have all experienced. There were moments in Little Rock in 1957 when I felt sure that the mood behind that sentiment was like my own. But in the same book was the consoling reference "When I meditate on Thee in the night watches, in the shadow of Thy wings will I rejoice." (Psalms 63:7)

Then there are the words of Paul addressed to his beloved young friend, Timothy, that seem particularly relevant to our times, "God has not given us the spirit of fear; but of power and of love and of a sound mind." (II Timothy 1:7)

Finally, in this same point the note of triumph: "Fear not, little flock; for it is your Father's good pleasure to give you the kingdom." (Luke 12:32)

꠶꠶ ꠷꠷

BROOKS HAYS, Special Assistant to President Kennedy, was introduced to politics and public affairs at an early age. His first active part in politics came shortly after he graduated from law school in 1922 when he helped manage his father's unsuccessful campaign for the same Congressional seat he himself was later to win. That same year he was elected secretary of the Arkansas State Democratic Convention, the youngest man ever to hold that position.

During his years of law practice and political activity in Arkansas, Mr. Hays became intensely interested in social work and became a recognized authority on farm tenancy in the South.

He has long fought for the extension of educational and economic opportunities for Negroes in the South and has taken active part in interracial organizations. After going to Congress he continued his interest in this complex problem. In a *February 2, 1949* address on the House floor, Representative Hays outlined the Arkansas Plan to extend full civil rights to minority groups without sacrificing the historic principles and traditions of any geographical section of the nation.

It was this interest in building bridges of understanding between the races that led him to arrange the Newport Conference between Governor Faubus and President Eisenhower at the time of the Little Rock school desegregation crisis.

Mr. Hays, a well-known churchman, served two terms (1957-1959) as President of the Southern Baptist Convention.

He is much in demand as a speaker on topics of special interest to church, civic, and college groups. He is regarded as one of the best storytellers in the United States and has come to be regarded by many Washington newsmen as one of the most prominent successors along these lines to Alben Barkley.

Mr. Hays was elected to the Seventy-eighth Congress in 1942 and was re-elected to succeeding Congresses through the Eighty-fifth.

Following his defeat for re-election, he was named to the Tennessee Valley Authority board of directors by President Eisenhower in 1959. He served in this post until 1961 when President Kennedy appointed him Assistant Secretary of State for Congressional Relations and then Special Assistant to the President.

Except the Lord build the house they labor in vain that build it.

PSALMS 127:1A *King James Version*

DR. BEN M. HERBSTER

President, United Church of Christ

THIS SETS FORTH in unmistakable terms the true relationship between the work of God and the labors of men.
Neither is exaggerated out of proportion. Both are recognized as essential.

It is very easy for us who give ourselves over to work
within the Church and to labor for the benefit of our fel-

lowmen to get the idea that everything rests upon our shoulders, that whether an event is for good or ill depends solely upon us. It is easy for us to think that we are "God's great gift to humanity" and that everything rests upon our labor. This gives us an exaggerated opinion of our own importance and breaks down the humility that all of us ought to hold within our hearts.

On the other hand, to believe that everything depends upon God is to cause a man to sit down, fold his hands and reject the responsibility that is rightfully his. It is to cause a man to believe he is less than he is. After all God has complimented men highly in choosing them to be His agents, to be the ones through whom He blesses the world. The truth is that for the most part God does not work out His blessings except through men. We may not be much but we are the ones through whom God sends His help and His redeeming message.

In this Psalm the right balance is struck. God first. Without Him we are lost. Our work accomplishes nothing. All we do is in vain. On the other hand, we have our part. The building has been left to us, the work has been committed to us. We do have our share and, in the main, God limits His work to what He can do through us.

"Except the Lord build the house, they labor in vain who build it."

Without God our building comes to naught. But God does not offer His help and power to the world except through the labor of our hands.

We are only men, not God. But we *are* men and we need to use that manhood, that strength for His cause. How better could one express it than, "Except the Lord build the house, they labor in vain who build it"?

>>> <<<

BEN MOHR HERBSTER, the first president of the 2,000,000-member United Church of Christ was a key figure in the development of that church body.

[104]

The Church was formed in 1957 by a union of the Evangelical and Reformed Church and the Congregational Christian Churches — both bodies themselves the result of earlier mergers. Until the constitution was declared in force in 1961, Dr. Herbster was a co-president of the constituting body.

The red-haired, soft-spoken, and genial churchman took up the Presidency after what he refers to as a "singularly unsensational" 30-year pastorate (1931-1961) at the Zion Evangelical and Reformed Church in Norwood, Ohio, a suburb of Cincinnati. Nevertheless, it was the leadership he demonstrated as a pastor along with his pioneering activity in the cause of Protestant unity that helped put Dr. Herbster at the helm of the merged church body.

Young Ben, who had worked in his father's hardware store and had at one time run a gas station in his Ohio home town, decided to become a minister while a student at Heidelberg College. His alma mater, of which he is a trustee, later awarded him an honorary degree as have several other colleges.

In addition to playing an active role in bringing the United Church of Christ into being, Dr. Herbster has long been identified with church unity groups and is a former President of the Cincinnati Council of Churches. He also has been an exchange preacher for the National Council and the British Council of Churches.

The church leader now lives in White Plains, N. Y., but he manages occasionally to visit the 275-acre Ohio farm he owns jointly with his sister. From it, he has said, they manage to make a "modest profit" in grain crops and support seventy-five head of Aberdeen Angus cattle.

O Lord, you have been our refuge through all generations.

*And may the gracious care
of the Lord our God be ours;
prosper the work of our hands for us!
Prosper the work of our hands!*

PSALMS 90:1 . . . 17* *Confraternity Version*

* Only the first and last verses are shown here, since the entire passage cannot be encompassed on the page.

CONRAD HILTON

President, Hilton Hotels

MY FAVORITE BIBLE TEXT is the Ninetieth Psalm, a prayer
that so beautifully expresses the dependence of man on
God. It has a very special significance to me, for the in-
cisiveness of its passages provided much of the inspiration
for the text of the pictorial presentation of "America On
Its Knees."

In 1950, I made my first venture into public speaking with a speech entitled "The Battle for Freedom" before the National Conference of Christians and Jews. In this speech, I called for a reawakening of our love of, and faith in, God. In the months that followed, many letters arrived commenting on my talk. One among these reached deeply within me. It was from a 12-year-old boy .who said he agreed with me that "our faith in God is our only hope." He asked for a reply to his letter.

Shortly, thereafter, I was on a train for Chicago and was thinking about the boy's letter. I saw a cartoon in a daily paper entitled, "When Problems Overwhelm." It depicted a portrait of Abraham Lincoln speaking to a harassed Uncle Sam saying, "Have you tried prayer, Sam?" To me that was confirmation of my vision. I went to New York to talk with friends who encouraged me to proceed. In the spirit of humility and with loving advice, a prayer took form. It applied the ancient wisdom of the Ninetieth Psalm to the modern day need for America to have unflinching faith in God.

Because I felt the need of re-expressing the belief of America's founders in prayer as a vital force in national life, on July Fourth, 1952, I published in some magazines a full-color pictorial presentation of "America On Its Knees." Uncle Sam was freely and confidently kneeling, knowing how to do battle for peace, and by his side this prayer. Within 24 hours after this printing, thousands upon thousands of letters came to my desk — 27,000 in one day! Letters from nearly every country in the world, from each state of our union, from all walks of life, affirmed the fact that the final victory in the battle for peace will rest with God.

Since then, the prayer and the Ninetieth Psalm have been constant companions of my life. They have brought sustenance to my soul during periods of international crisis over the last decade. I am repeatedly buoyed up by letters that continually arrive from persons throughout the Free

World commenting on "America On Its Knees." It is this consensus of faith, from the heart of America, which demonstrates the national unity and purpose of our citizens.

→》》-《《←

CONRAD HILTON, head of the world's leading hotel organization (some 34,000 rooms in 49 hotels in the United States and abroad) is noted for his uncommon flair for hotel purchase and management. This flair has carried him to the top where he is known as host to millions of travelers.

Starting with a small hotel in Cisco, Texas, in 1919, the size and importance of Mr. Hilton's operations has increased through the years. Up to the time he acquired the Statler Hotels in 1954, he was known to the trade as "the man who bought the Waldorf"—a high compliment since this is one of the world's most famous hotels, and owning it is considered an ultimate symbol of success in the field.

Mr. Hilton is chairman of the board and president of the Hilton Hotels Corporation with total assets of more than $231,000,000 as compared to some $51,000,000 when the corporation was formed in 1946.

This host to the world has the energy and drive of a man of 50 — or someone 20 years younger than he. He is affable and possessed of a disarming candor along with an unaffected cosmopolitan manner.

Six-foot-two Conrad Hilton is an active golfer, a tireless dancer, and a first-rate pianist. Friends describe him as a man who works and plays with equal flair — and one who is tenacious in pursuing a deal.

In recent years, Mr. Hilton has become increasingly active in national and world affairs. His public addresses on such subjects as the United Europe movement, the growing menace of Communism, and the need for morality and leadership in government have been widely circulated and quoted. When he gave the address, "The Battle for Freedom," the National Conference of Christian and Jews presented him with its annual Brotherhood Award. He received a Freedoms Foundation award for the speech, "Blueprint for Freedom."

[109]

For God so loved the world, that he gave his only begotten Son, that whosoever believeth in him should not perish, but have everlasting life.

JOHN 3:16 *King James Version*

JEROME HINES

The Metropolitan Opera Company

THIS SCRIPTURE VERSE has been so often quoted that I hesitated to write concerning it on this occasion. But, indeed, my life would be desolate without its glorious promise.

Time after time, whether in my personal life or in my career, I have found myself literally swamped by the circumstances surrounding me. Yet time after time I, as many others, have turned to the promise of God contained in this verse and have once again felt the solid Rock beneath my feet instead of the floor of life's cares, especially at the times when in my own Christian walk I have stumbled and fallen short of His glory.

For in this verse is the blessed assurance that we weak mortals, with our feet of clay exemplifying anything but holy perfection, can yet aspire to His kingdom and His love through simple faith. That Jesus died for each and every one of us that we may live, is breathed out of every line of the Bible. Yet nowhere is it so clearly shown as in this verse.

How often when I have found myself sunken in despair, or doubt, have I been lifted again by the sure knowledge that my salvation is God's doing, not my own. My deeds cannot save me, only His atoning sacrifice on the Cross. When this realization sinks home again and again I cease my struggles and yield the problems to Him.

And at the times when I feel particularly barren of love for those about me, this verse reminds me that He loved me while I was still in my sin. How can I withhold love from another when Jesus died for him too. It is only when I am filled with Him that I have my full capacity to love.

I suppose that this verse means as much to me as any other I have ever read for it contains all the essential elements of Christianity and Jesus Christ its divine author, the principle one being God's love, seeking and sacrifice for that which was lost.

And that was *me*.

➤➤➤ ◄◄◄

JEROME HINES says that ever since he wrote the religious opera, *I Am The Way* he has been a changed man — what he calls a "born-again Christian."

Nowadays, when he is not performing on the stage of the Metropolitan Opera Company in New York City, the six-foot-seven-inch native of California can often be found in a

Bowery mission, singing hymns in his resounding bass. On tour with the Metropolitan after one of his famous performances in *Don Giovanni, Boris Godunoff* or as Mephistopheles in *Faust,* he may conduct a Bible class for members of the company or search out a mission to see if they will let him sing a gospel song or give a testimonial to Christ.

I Am The Way is the first part of a projected trilogy of music dramas based on the life of Christ, in which the author sings the part of the Lord. In 1950 Mr. Hines decided to do the Passion play in operatic form. As a result, he was exposed to more and more reading of Scriptures, "and they began to have their effect on me."

Mr. Hines says that after about three years of working on the opera, he had a "series of experiences which converted me."

One night in 1953 when he was struggling with the theme of the Holy Spirit — the music that was to go under the spoken words of the Sermon on the Mount — Mr. Hines felt that he couldn't do it. "Funny thing, I didn't believe in a personal God at that time; yet I found myself asking God to help me. And that evening, through the music, I literally received the Holy Spirit for the first time."

≫≫ ≫≫ ≫≫ ≫≫ ≫≫ ≫≫ ≫≫ ≫≫ ≫≫ ≫≫ ≫≫ ≪≪ ≪≪ ≪≪ ≪≪ ≪≪ ≪≪ ≪≪ ≪≪ ≪≪ ≪≪ ≪≪

Beloved, I wish above all things that thou mayest prosper and be in health, even as thy soul prospereth.

JOHN 3:2 *King James Version*

HERSCHEL H. HOBBS

Pastor, First Baptist Church, Oklahoma City, Oklahoma
President, Southern Baptist Convention

JESUS SAID, "I am come that they might have life, and that they might have it more abundantly" (John 10:10). "Abundantly" means "overflowing all the edges around." The abundant life is the overflowing life. We bless others by the overflow. The Christian's life should be filled to overflowing with a perfect balance of those elements that not only bless him, but that make him a blessing.

Three ideas prevail as to the nature of man: he is a body only; he is both body and soul; he is a soul and has a body. The New Testament repudiates the first, recognizes the truth contained in the second, but places greater emphasis on the third. "For what is a man profited, if he shall gain the whole world, and lose his own soul?" (Matt. 16:26). The answer to this question is contained in III John 2.

There is no teaching in the New Testament which denies to man the legitimate desire for and the pursuit of material prosperity and bodily health. Quite the contrary is true. But it does warn against making these things an end unto themselves. Only as prosperity and health are balanced by the prosperity of the soul can one rightly enjoy and employ the former in keeping with God's will and purpose.

Our generation desperately needs to realize and experience this truth. We are an age that is geared to time but forgetful of the eternal. Through the pursuit of prosperity and health, we live better and longer. But we are in danger of losing the meaning of life itself.

The word "prosper" means to have a good journey. To have a good journey in material and physical things alone is to lose our way. If the journey through life, and beyond, is to be good indeed, we must permit our souls to catch up with our bodies. For this reason we never tire of wishing for all men:

"Beloved, I wish above all things that thou mayest prosper and be in health, even as thy soul prospereth."

-»»-«««-

H. H. HOBBS holds or has held major offices with many agencies of the more-than-ten-million-member Southern Baptist Convention, of which he served two terms as President (1961-63), but he considers his true vocation to be that of pastor.

[116]

He has said, "I think that the preaching, believing, and applying of the Gospel of Jesus Christ is the solution to all our problems."

Dr. Hobbs has held eight pulpits since he was ordained in Birmingham, Alabama, in 1929. He became pastor of Oklahoma City's First Baptist Church in 1949. He believes that a pulpit ministry is a challenge. And he feels that pastoral work provides him with the deepest satisfaction because of the personal relationships that are involved.

His pulpit ministry has been extended since 1958 through round-the-world radio broadcasts on the weekly "Baptist Hour" carried by 484 stations to the most remote regions of the earth — a service he renders without· remuneration.

Dr. Hobb's avocation is writing. Since 1951 he has written 14 books on Biblical and evangelistic subjects, two of which have been translated in Portuguese and one in Spanish.

He is widely in demand as a speaker throughout this country. He has held evangelistic meetings in Japan and Korea and has conducted a Bible Study Tour to the Holy Land.

The Lord bless thee, and keep thee: . . .
and give thee peace.
NUMBERS 6:24-26 *King James Version*

HERBERT HOOVER

Thirty-first President of The United States of America

HERBERT HOOVER'S name has long been associated with peace.

It was characteristic of America's eldest statesman, even though convalescing at the time this book was being prepared, that he sent words of peace as his contribution.

His many public services have reflected the Quaker-instilled philosophy of peace. His name and work are honored throughout Europe for his missions there after two world wars. He was food administrator of the relief program in Belgium. And President Truman called on him to coordinate world food supplies during a time of severe famine and later to help Germany and Austria rebuild industrially and otherwise.

Despite his concern with many serious projects — and with authoring some 30 books, 26 of them since he left the White House in 1933 — the former President has never lost his interest in sports. And he still manages to fit into his busy schedule a fishing excursion on his boat, *Captiva*.

In recent years, the Boys Clubs of America have been a major interest. Under his leadership as board chairman, the organization has increased from 130 to 526 units working with boys who for the most part come from depressed surroundings.

Many a youngster writing him (his mail is enormous, with out-going mail totaling more than 45,000 pieces in a year's time) has received a reply from Mr. Hoover in which he expresses a bit of philosophy in terms a boy or girl can understand.

Mr. Hoover has been given some 468 medals, awards, and honors. And he has been awarded 85 honorary degrees — a record collection probably not matched by any other individual.

The former engineer-turned-public-servant amassed a fortune at an early age. As a consequence he was financially able and personally motivated to — as he has put it — "do something for his country" by never accepting pay of any kind for his public services. Often, he has even paid his traveling expenses. His salaries earned as President and in other Government jobs were turned over intact by Mr. Hoover to be used for charities and public-service projects.

Mr. Hoover is still very alert to the problems of the world and aware of the threats to this nation's way of life. But he believes in the future because he believes in the people of America.

Belief in God — he has said — is America's priceless advantage over her enemies.

I said, I will take heed to my ways, that I sin not with my tongue: I will keep my mouth with a bridle, while the wicked is before me.

O spare me, that I may recover strength, before I go hence, and be no more.

PSALMS 39:1 . . . 13* *King James Version*

*Only the first and last verses are shown here, since the entire passage cannot be encompassed on the page.

FANNIE HURST

Writer

THIS PSALM OF DAVID asks, rather than proclaims, with surety. Along with those of us to whom immortality is a hope, rather than a conviction, he queries: "Lord, make me to know mine end, and the measure of my days, what it is; that I may know how frail I am.

"And now, Lord, what wait I for?"

Then that crashing last line: "O spare me, that I may recover strength, before I go hence, and be no more."

Obviously, David is beset by the uncertainties shared by those of us who have not yet come into the inheritance of assurance of immortality.

Wadsworth says with calm conviction: "Though inland far we be, our souls have sight of that immortal seal which brought us hither."

But David in the wilderness of his confusions cries: Spare me before I go hence and be no more."

Even in his fullness in the faith of God he seems to draw up sharply before the overpowering immensity of the, or a, beyond.

He does not query whither, but states declaratively "Before I go and be no more."

Yet somewhere inherent within him must have been doubts of that extreme finality. Along with the immemorial conjectures of mortals, he must have cried out within himself: this inch of time between birth and death, man's span of life cannot be all.

The veins in a leaf, the coming of a dawn, oceans rushing up to kiss the land, the grandeur of birth, the symphonic rhythm of the scheme of seasons — surely David must have cried out this cannot be the all. . . .

Yet how comforting that even he seems to share the wonderments and uncertainties of those of us who grope.

FANNIE HURST has created dozens of electric characters who will live in the memory of millions who have read her books — Ray Schmidt of *Back Street*, Bertha in *Lummox*, Mamma of *Humoresque*, to name a few — but none of them is as intriguing an individual as the creator herself.

Miss Hurst is an enthusiastic woman of many facets and vast energies — a world citizen. If she had a coat of arms, her device would consist of a single lily. She wears a large jeweled lily at her throat and signs her letters to her intimate friends with a sketch of a lily instead of her name. She explains her love for the flower by saying, "Its elaborate simplicity achieves complete beauty in one gesture."

"The Lady of the Lilies" is a Manhattanite in the truest sense. A gregarious person, she moves with equal enthusiasm in a variety of circles — from Park Avenue to the Bowery. In fact, Miss Hurst is only happy in Manhattan. She loves its shops, its slums, its skyscrapers and the people who inhabit them.

Overflowing with energy despite her herculean literary labors (she has written 17 novels, several plays and innumerable short stories), Miss Hurst finds time for myriad civic and social activities.

But the key to the real Fannie Hurst lies in her work. She writes forcefully and with infinite understanding of the human heart.

Is not this the fast that I have chosen?
To loose the fetters of wickedness,
To undo the bands of the yoke,
And to let the oppressed go free,
And that ye break every yoke?
Is it not to deal thy bread to the hungry,
And that thou bring the poor that are cast
out to thy house?
When thou seest the naked, that thou
cover him,
And that thou hide not thyself from thine
own flesh?
Then shall thy light break forth as the
morning
And thy healing shall spring forth speedily;
And thy righteousness shall go before thee,
The glory of the Lord shall be thy reward.

ISAIAH 58:6-8 *Masoretic Text*

MRS. CHARLES HYMES

President, National Council of Jewish Women

FROM THE TIME I was a youngster in religious school, this particular passage embodied for me everything that Judaism means, as well as what I truly have considered the goal and objectives of my life.

My mother used to say to her four children, "Remember the dollar is round and it rolls. Judge people by what they are and do, not by their social position or worldly goods."

She also had a scorn for people who went piously through the motions of religious observance but treated their fellow men shabbily. Although she attended services very regularly, her attitude was that this was only a part of our responsibility in relation to Judaism. We fasted on Yom Kippur — the Day of Atonement — but she constantly reminded us that this was only for the purpose of making us conscious of the need to make some sacrifice at all times for our fellow men.

As I grew up, two concepts of life became deeply embodied within me; one, the concept of freedom, the other, our responsibility to our fellow men.

Were man to "undo the bonds of the yoke" and to deal his bread to the hungry, we would not have to agonize about the freedom or security of mankind. Then all our remarkable scientific discoveries and achievements that now are aimed primarily for the potential destruction of men — our space exploration — our nuclear fission — all these wonders of our universe could indeed be used for the benefit of all humanity.

-->> <<--

MRS. CHARLES HYMES' record of public service as President (1959-63) of the National Council of Jewish Women is in many ways a model of that organization's motto of "faith and humanity" and its belief in "education and service."

As a young school teacher just out of the University of Minnesota, Mrs. Hymes became a leader in citizen-activity for the improvement of public education in Minnesota. The Citizens' Committee for Public Education, which she helped found, was the first of its kind in the United States and served to inspire many others later organized in all parts of the country.

Through the National Council of Jewish Women, Mrs. Hymes continued to work for better education and broader welfare services. She is a member of the Board of Governors of Hebrew University in Jerusalem and a vice president of the International Council of Jewish Women, which has groups in 18 countries.

In addition Mrs. Hymes has devoted a life of service to other fields such as mental health, educational television, and literary education for adults. An attractive woman with a straightforward manner, she gets to the heart of a subject right away. Her interests in education have brought her to the attention of various high State and Federal governmental officials who have appointed her to a number of important posts and committees. President Kennedy named Mrs. Hymes to the newly-formed Commission on the Status of Women.

She comes by way of her responsibilities "naturally" — since her whole family has always been involved in civic affairs. And Mrs. Hymes continues her many religious and civic activities as a woman with "a very important stake in the future." As she puts it, "I have five grandchildren and, after all, the kind of world they live in is very important to me."

If there be therefore any consolation in
   Christ, if any comfort of love, if any
   fellowship of the Spirit, if any bowels
   and mercies, fulfil ye my joy, that ye be
   likeminded, having the same love, being
   of one accord, of one mind.
Let this mind be in you, which was also in
   Christ Jesus: who, being in the form of
   God, thought it not robbery to be
   equal with God: but made himself of
   no reputation, and took upon him the
   form of a servant, and was made in the
   likeness of men: and being found in
   fashion as a man he humbled himself,
   and became obedient unto death, even
   the death of the cross. Wherefore God
   also hath highly exalted him, and
   given him a name which is above every
   name; that at the name of Jesus every
   knee should bow, of things in
   heaven, and things in earth, and things
   under the earth; and that every tongue
   should confess that Jesus Christ is
   Lord, to the glory of God the Father.

PHILLIPIANS 2:1-2,5-11 *King James Version*

ARCHBISHOP IAKOVOS

*Archbishop of the Greek Orthodox Archdiocese
of North and South America.*

THIS PASSAGE from the Epistle of Paul the Apostle to the
Phillipians illuminates the true nature of Christian oneness
with unequaled clarity. It makes plain that oneness is the
basis for both unity and union. It stresses that no unity of
purpose is possible or no union or reunion of the Church

can ever be effected unless it is both motivated and nourished by oneness of mind, of love and charity, of soul and of Christian conscience.

This is my favorite biblical passage for yet another reason. It depicts and projects in a most heartwarming light the true Christ, the real Son of God, the genuine character of His coming to the world. The God-made man cannot be the heir of heaven unless he gives up his all, and serves his fellow man in the likeness of Jesus with humility and sacrificial spirit. To respond to the calling of our Christian past is the only way in which Christians may be more securely linked in an unbroken unity with one another and with Christ.

This is the intent of Paul's famous words quoted above.

⊸≫⧫≪⊷

IAKOVOS, the Archbishop of the Greek Orthodox Church of North and South America since 1959 is known as a leader of the present-day ecumenical movement for Christian unity and has been described as "a breath of fresh air in Eastern Orthodoxy in this country."

The bearded, distinguished-looking prelate is aware of and well-versed in church problems. A man possessed of great warmth, he is as cooperative with individuals as he is with Christian church bodies that share in the quest for unity.

The Archbishop, who is an American citizen with headquarters in New York City came to this country in 1939 from Istanbul and served his Church after his ordination in various cities and in increasingly higher positions. In 1954 he was elected Bishop of Melita (Malta) and the following year he was appointed Representative of the Ecumenical Patriarchate of the World Council of Churches headquarters in Geneva. Four years later he was elected Archbishop.

As the Geneva Representative of the Ecumenical Patriarchate, Archbishop Iakovos (then known as Metropolitan James)

[132]

traveled extensively throughout the world and attended many ecclesiastical meetings and councils. He also visited the United States on several occasions and delivered lectures at Harvard, Boston University, and other institutions and at various religious conferences. He is the author of many religious books and pamphlets.

The Archbishop has close ties with Protestant and Episcopal groups in the United States, especially within the World and National Councils of Churches. He is serving his second term as a President of the World Council.

The Greek Archdiocese, which Iakovos heads, is under the jurisdiction of the ancient Ecumenical Patriarchate of Constantinople. The Archdiocese has 1,500,000 communicants and 380 churches in the United States and is the headquarters of the Greek Orthodox Church, which is the largest of the many Eastern Orthodox bodies in America.

*Master, which is the great commandment
in the law? Jesus said unto him,
Thou shalt love the Lord thy God with
all thy heart, and with all thy soul, and
with all thy mind. This is the first and
great commandment. And the second is
like unto it, Thou shalt love thy
neighbour as thyself. On these two
commandments hang all the law and
the prophets.*

MATTHEW 22:36-40 *King James Version*

DR. LEWIS W. JONES

President, The National Conference of Christians and Jews

IN THIS STATEMENT Jesus makes unmistakably clear the great affirmation that all men must make. We must cast aside all idols and tribal gods and superstitions in devotion to the one God of the universe. This is the everlasting "aye" — "the will to believe" — "the ultimate concern."

[135]

The second commandment to love thy neighbour requires first that man — made in the image of God — must have dignity and self-respect before he can properly love his neighbour. Thus the dignity of man derives from the love of God and unites all mankind in a brotherhood of mutual love and respect.

The first and second commandments are the fulfillment of Jewish religious experience and create a common bond between Christians and Jews. They encompass and transcend all religious wisdom.

⇢⇠

DR. LEWIS WEBSTER JONES accepted the presidency of the National Conference of Christians and Jews in 1958. Those who knew him well were not surprised, for the central focus of Dr. Jones' career as educator, university president and governmental adviser, over the past three decades, had been upon public affairs and social welfare.

In many addresses, articles and reviews during that period, he enunciated his strong conviction about the vital interplay of religion and politics in our American democracy and called for the translation of religious and moral principles into practical civic action.

For eight years prior to becoming president of NCCJ, Dr. Jones headed Rutgers University and supervised its reorganization into a state university. From 1947 to 1951 he was president of the University of Arkansas (which he integrated and which is still integrated), and from 1932 until 1947 he was at Bennington College, first as an economics professor and later, for six years, as president.

During these years, Dr. Jones was in and out of Washington almost continually on many important special assignments for the United States Government. An expert mediator, he was enlisted to settle labor disputes in vital industries New England during World War II. Later, Dr. Jones served as a member of various Presidential commissions.

If thou canst believe, all things are possible to him that believeth.

MARK 9:23 *King James Version*

HENRY J. KAISER

Industrialist-Builder

TIMES BEYOND NUMBER, I have experienced the proof of
the words of Jesus that "all things are possible to him that
believeth."

Believing means faith, and I have seen it demonstrated
again and again that faith is a key to accomplishment and
to attaining the greatest and most satisfying values in life.

[139]

Faith in God answers the questions and longings of your soul — gives you help from the Higher Source — and sees the workings of the Creator in everything.

Faith in your fellowmen — whom you love and want to serve and whose needs you seek to help fill — adds to the purpose and driving power of your work in life.

Faith in yourself and your highest aspirations releases your creative inner powers.

"If thou canst believe" — if you have faith in your dreams, you can make them come true, providing you really work at them. For "Faith without works is dead."

What a man can imagine or conceive with mind and heart, he can accomplish. "Impossibles" are only impossibles as thinking makes them so. Faith can unleash the power that enables you to accomplish whatever is right that you set out to do.

Faith generates a wider and wider circle of faith.

Yet faith can't be turned on and off like a faucet — Turned on to make dollars and turned off in our relations with God and our fellowmen.

Each human being needs to give a chance not only to the divine spark of spirit within himself, but to see it in others.

Faith in God leads to the fullest life. . . . We can find God wherever we turn our insight. God speaks through "the flower in the crannied wall," through the beauty of a garden or a flaming sunset, through every mystery of life, through the wonder of a child, and through the spirits of fellowmen created in His image.

For each individual, the paramount need is to develop within himself the rounded faith without which nothing *really* worthwhile is accomplished.

Paul wrote in his Epistle to the Philippians, 4:13: "I can do all things through Christ which strengtheneth me."

To men and women of faith, resolved to give to their lives and to their fellowmen the finest that is within themselves, I would suggest this prayerful meditation:

[140]

May each of us keep vision clear to see life's goals;
May each use the inner power of spirit:
Live every day by faith —
Faith to keep thought and action good within God's sight,
Faith to believe one's finest dreams,
Faith to triumph over fear,
Faith in peace and brotherhood for all God's children.
Fill each day with service . . . courage . . . purpose —
Knowing as Christ has taught:
"All things are possible to him that believeth."

⇒≫-≪⇐

HENRY J. KAISER, the famed shipbuilder of World War II, began his business career at 13 when he left school to take a $1.50-a-week job as cash boy for a Utica, N. Y., dry goods store. He was a son of German immigrants. Mr. Kaiser later traveled as a salesman and at 22 became a junior partner of a photographic firm, which a year later he purchased and expanded.

Between the purchase of his first business and World War II, Mr. Kaiser had established in 1914 his first business at 32, had carried out millions of dollars worth of highway construction in the Pacific Northwest and California, and had reached what he considers the turning point in his life — a $20,000,000 (huge for 1927) highway and bridge building program in Cuba — that led to partnerships and associations with other contractors for cooperative bidding and construction on gigantic projects.

Mr. Kaiser has also established an international reputation in a non-business area — health and medical care. The Kaiser Foundation, a non-profit, charitable trust operating on the West Coast and in Hawaii, is the result of more than 20 years' pioneering to bring high quality medical care within financial reach of the average man.

In the world you have tribulation; but be of good cheer, I have overcome the world.

JOHN 16:33 *Revised Standard Version*

BISHOP GERALD KENNEDY

Bishop, The Los Angeles Area, The Methodist Church

THESE GALLANT WORDS spoken by One who is facing death are to me one of the high points of the Bible. They are both a promise and a spur, and I have found them the words I needed to hear in many a difficult situation.

Jesus is saying to us that we live in the world and that we are not to expect any escape from it. There is nothing here of acting as if the world did not exist. We are in the world and we are going to have trouble. Unlike so many other leaders, Jesus never promised his disciples an easy time or a comfortable living. He puts it very bluntly and simply states that trouble is a part of the experience of men who live in this world and follow him.

But he bids his followers to be of good cheer. We may try to get through the difficulties of our lives by drinking alcohol. Or we may form mutual admiration societies and tell ourselves how good we are. We think we can pretend and by the sheer power of our wishing make our life easier. But Jesus gives us some good cheer which the world can neither give nor understand. I have seen it shining in the faces of Christians behind the Iron Curtain as they listened to the Scriptures read and sang a hymn. It has been apparent through the centuries and has manifested itself in a kind of absurd joy in the midst of suffering and difficulty. I have found it in the lives of the quiet saints who carry their heavy burdens with grace and who face their sorrows with dignity and assurance. One of his greatest gifts is good cheer in the midst of tribulation.

And all of this is possible because we know that He has overcome the world. He has changed civilizations and he has performed miracles in human life. It comes to us at last that God will have the final word and that he will make the final decision. So these words have been like a trumpet of hope to me through the years and I could never describe adequately how often they have kept me on my feet.

※ ※

BISHOP GERALD KENNEDY is one of the great Christian leaders of mid-twentieth century America and one of the ablest, most forthright and challenging spokesmen of American Protestantism. That he should command such a position is due, in large measure, to a rare combination of talents as preacher, administrator and writer.

The imprint of his leadership already has been left in unmistakable ways upon his chief concern, overseeing the Southern California-Arizona Methodist Conference and Hawaii Mission, with their 450 churches, 230,000 members and nearly 800 ministers.

Many have paid tribute to Bishop Kennedy. *Newsweek* (March 28, 1955) listed him among ten of the greatest American preachers. *Time* (April 11, 1960) called him a "tireless circuit rider," who amid all his travels and duties can be pungently articulate. And *Pulpit Digest* said, "knowing him is the best medicine for any pessimism about where the Church is headed."

But the one tribute that stands out, was from a long-time friend and colleague. When Bishop Kennedy took office as president of the Methodist Council of Bishops, Bishop G. Bromley Oxnam said of him: "He is the most gifted churchman I know in speech, writing and reading. He is vital, alive to everything that is alive. But he cannot tolerate the obvious. His judgment will not allow his love to keep him from doing his duty. He has great intelligence. In his preaching, he takes off from the place where I thought he would conclude. This man is different. He makes religion real."

*In righteousness shalt thou be established;
thou shalt be far from oppression . . .
And all thy children shall be taught
of the Lord . . . (Then) my kindness
shall not depart from thee, neither shall
the covenant of my peace be removed.*

ISAIAH 54:14, 13, 10 *King James Version*

OSCAR M. LAZRUS

Chairman of the Board, Benrus Watch Company, Inc.

OUR LIVES ARE BESET by difficulties in our personal relations, in our anxieties regarding this world tension in which we find ourselves, in our struggle to create and maintain our place in society. Alone and unaided we cannot triumph; but with God's help, all things are possible. If we would but

pray sincerely and put our faith in One greater than ourselves, we might be shown the way. If we continue to have
faith and do the right (as God gives us to see that right),
He will unfold to us His purposes in His own good time,
and we will realize that God has worked out for us our
salvation through the humble doings of our daily life.

Life has given me, as it has all of us, much happiness
and much sorrow. I may not always understand God's
purposes, but I can be always thankful for the salvation of
work and service to others that He places before me. He
tells us, "Keep ye judgements and do justice: for my salvation is near to come, and my righteousness to be re-
vealed." (Mark 56:1)

Actually sacrifice and work to extend economic and
social righteousness universally, as well as liberty from oppression, are the individual's avenues to the care and peace
that God promised to each person. "In righteousness shalt
thou be established; thou shalt be far from oppression . . .
And all thy children shall be taught of the Lord . . . (Then)
my kindness shall not depart from thee, neither shall the
covenant of my peace be removed." (Isaiah 54:14, 13, 10)

This passage was never as relevant for as many people
as it is in our time. It is a prescription for freedom from
terror and union for security long before Man's political,
economic, and social institutions evolved to what they are
in all nations today. It offers us hope in a turbulent, revo-
lutionary era.

⇥≫ ≪⇤

OSCAR M. LAZRUS is a big businessman who is always ready
to blast away at any big businessmen who he feels are exploit-
ing the people. In his passionate devotion to ideals of social justice and social welfare, he speaks his mind and lets the chips fall

where they may. "I believe in the welfare state," he says to the dismay of many of his fellow corporation chiefs. "People talk about a man providing for education, sickness, and old age through his own savings — many a thrifty hard-working man is lucky to save $200 in his whole life."

Mr. Lazrus puts his ideals into practice. When he was president of a Jewish-supported hospital located in Harlem, he successfully fought a proposal to move the hospital and merge it with a Jewish hospital in another neighborhood. He admitted the location was inconvenient to the Jewish residents of the city, but "those people in the neighborhood needed that hospital." Mr. Lazrus is delegate-at-large to the Federation of Jewish Philanthropies, a job he jokingly suggests he was given because none of the agencies that make up the Federation was willing to take on his social zeal. He is also National Secretary of The National Conference of Christians and Jews and an executive in three other service organizations.

Mr. Lazrus has always taken his feeling for the rights of the common man for granted. "I suppose it's in the blood," he says recalling an uncle who joined an anarchist colony. Mr. Lazrus's parents brought him to the United States from Rumania when he was an infant. He is proud of his immigrant heritage. "They talk of the courage of the pioneers who opened the West. To bring eight children to a strange country where you don't know a word of the language — that's courage too."

Mr. Lazrus grew up on Manhattan's Lower East Side, where he had plenty of opportunity to develop his social conscience. He left a three-dollar-a-week job in an embroidery factory to work in a law office six days a week for six dollars. He studied law while working in the Brooklyn Finance Department and finally hung out his shingle. He was a successful lawyer by the time he and his two brothers launched a watch importing company following World War I. The company became the Benrus Watch Company, one of America's largest. Mr. Lazrus is now chairman of the board and his two Harvard-educated sons are president and executive vice president.

Why did a man who identifies himself with the common man become a wealthy businessman? "I wanted to guard myself from the wealthy," he says with a winning smile.

[149]

But the God of all grace, who hath called us unto his eternal glory by Christ Jesus, after that ye have suffered a while, make you perfect, 'stablish, strengthen, and settle you.

PETER 1:5-10 *King James Version*

COMMISSIONER
NORMAN MARSHALL

National Commander of The Salvation Army in the U.S.A.

FOLLOWING THE CUSTOM OF MY FATHER, early in my study of God's Word I marked or underlined certain passages of Scripture that impressed me. In this way my eye would catch these verses again and again until they became indelibly written on my mind and I would find myself repeating them until the message in the Word gripped me.

Such was the experience with respect to this particular text, which has been called the "Fisherman's Benediction." Dr. Goodspeed has translated the verse in this way: "And God, the giver of all mercy, who through your union with Christ has called you to His eternal glory, after you have suffered a little while, will Himself make you perfect, steadfast, and strong."

We can quite understand how this confession welled up in Peter's heart when he remembered his unfaithfulness, his denial of his Lord and Master, his turning back from discipleship just when Jesus needed him most. But Peter also remembered the pity and forgiveness on the face of Jesus when He turned and looked upon him, and he "went out and wept bitterly." Following his repentance Peter's heart was comforted when he received the message of the women who had gone to the sepulcher and found it empty and were sent back to tell the disciples *"and Peter"* that Christ was risen and would meet them in Galilee. What joy and comfort came to Peter in the assurance of his forgiveness and reinstatement as one of Jesus' disciples! No wonder Peter in his benediction, at the close of his first letter to these early Christians, referred to God as the "God of all grace," or as Goodspeed put it, "God, the giver of all mercy."

Included in this benediction was not only the mercy of God, but also the "call" of God to us through Christ to share with Him His eternal glory, and the promise of God to each of us of His gracious ministry whereby we shall be made whole and complete in Him and established and strengthened in our new life in Christ.

Since we all have "sinned and come short of His glory" and have "turned everyone to his own way" and have denied our Lord and Master just like Peter did, this Fisherman's Benediction constitutes for all of us both a comfort and a challenge, and this text shall ever remain one of my favorite verses from the Word of God.

NORMAN S. MARSHALL, who became National Commander of The Salvation Army in the United States in September of 1957, came from Army stock. His father was a Canadian-born pioneer in The Salvation Army and his mother was a second-generation Salvationist.

One of five Marshall children to become officers, the Commissioner developed enthusiasm for the spirit of The Salvation Army as a boy. At 10 he was playing a cornet in the St. Louis Corps Band. In high school he was a part-time physical director in the Minneapolis YMCA.

After his commissioning as an officer, he held various posts in the Dakotas, served as private secretary to the Western Territorial Commander, participated in Salvation Army World War I work, and served as an Infantry Chaplain. These were the beginnings of his climb up through the ranks of officership — a climb that brought him assignments in all sections of the nation. He went to New York City in 1953 where he commanded the Eastern Territory until his appointment as National Commander.

As he approached the age of retirement, Commissioner Marshall had devoted nearly a half-century of service to people as a Salvation Army officer. A gentle man — but strong and persuasive in leadership and action — he still possesses the sturdy physical appearance of the athlete he once was as a high school student. In his dealings with people, he is a dramatic example of the dedication a Salvation Army officer gives "with his heart to God and hand to man."

The Commissioner has held many high Army positions other than his commands. He has served twice as a member of The Salvation Army High Council, the legal body that elects the General of The Salvation Army. He has visited Army operations in many countries. And he holds the Knight Commander of the Order of Vasa decoration from the King of Sweden for his services to the Swedish people in the United States.

Commissioner Marshall is active in ecumenical work and attended the New Delhi sessions of the World Council of Churches, of which he is a U.S. executive committee member. He is a member of and participates in various national social welfare and civic organizations, many of which elected him to high office.

In the beginning was the Word, and the Word was with God; and the Word was God. He was in the beginning with God. All things were made through him, and without him was made nothing that has been made. In him was life, and the life was the light of men. And the light shines in the darkness; and the darkness grasped it not.

And the Word was made flesh, and dwelt among us. And we saw his glory — glory as of the only-begotten of the Father — full of grace and of truth.

JOHN 1:1 ... 16 * *Douay Version*

* Only the first and last verses are shown here, since the entire passage cannot be encompassed on the page.

GEORGE MEANY

*President, American Federation of Labor
and Congress of Industrial Organizations*

MY FAVORITE BIBLE PASSAGE is the first chapter of the
Gospel according to St. John.

This Gospel concludes every celebration of the Holy
Sacrifice of the Mass. Traditionally, as we come to its last
words "as the Word was made flesh and dwelt amont us,"
we all kneel in reverence.

[155]

I have always felt that this Holy Gospel is one of the most beautiful and haunting passages in the Bible. To me, these verses have a meaning far beyond the actual words, and they give us much to ponder on.

-»»-«««-

GEORGE MEANY has his roots in the trade union movement. With it he has branched out into many fields, beyond wages and working conditions, which affect the welfare of the nation's workers.

He is considered an authority on national economic issues, social legislation, and international affairs. He has pioneered in moves to attain industrial peace and led in the fight for civil rights.

The leader of the American labor movement enjoys challenge. When a critical situation arises, he responds with energy, decisiveness, and what has been called an unerring instinct for the right course.

Using these talents, Mr. Meany helped to bring about the merger of the American Federation of Labor and Congress of Industrial Organizations in 1955 after 20 years of division and bitter rivalry. The merger was his first announced goal after becoming AFL President, and it represents what he belives to be his major achievement.

Mr. Meany is known as a "strong" man with a gift of and respect for the power of truth, which observers say he uses consistently and effectively.

For the past quarter of a century, he has sought with increasing success to broaden labor's horizons. Along with other trade union leaders, he recognized the folly of isolationism. Under his leadership, the American trade union movement has become an increasingly influential force in international affairs. Because of his contributions to world peace and freedom, Mr. Meany was twice named by President Eisenhower as a U.S. Delegate to the United Nations General Assembly.

George Meany is a native of New York City where, forced to leave high school because of family circumstances, he chose his father's trade: plumbing. Seven years after he had received his journeyman certificate in 1915, he was elected to his first trade union post. Thereafter the climb was rapid — from local to New York State Federation offices, from AFL Secretary-Treasurer to President in 1952 following the death of William Green.

In 1955, he was elected President of the combined AFL-CIO.

Let the words of my mouth and the meditation of my heart be acceptable in thy sight, O Lord, my strength, and my redeemer.

PSALMS 19:14 *King James Version*

PAUL MILLER

President, The Gannett Newspapers

THESE BIBLE WORDS — "Let the words of my mouth and the meditation of my heart be acceptable in thy sight, O Lord, my strength, and my redeemer" — are a favorite of my 82-year-old mother, who lives in Clarksville, Tenn., and continues active in the work of the Christian Church there.

My late father was a Christian Church minister in Oklahoma and Missouri.

I have often heard this verse repeated by my mother who, even with six children, read often to them, not only from the Bible but from contemporary literature, from history and from the classics.

This Bible quotation also is one of my favorites, and I have been helped by it. First, it teaches us to try to refrain from saying anything unbecoming for a Christian to say. Also, it teaches us to be mindful that God knows our innermost thoughts.

⫸⫷

PAUL MILLER'S journalistic career was launched when he was 15 years old. At that age, he won a national editorial writing contest, which he felt qualified him for a desk in a newspaper office. He got it — by hanging around the *Pawhuska* (Oklahoma) *Daily Journal* until they gave him a job. He was a reporter the next year, and by the time he went away to college at 18, he was the city editor.

After college, the young newspaperman was hired by The Associated Press in 1932. Thereafter for 15 years he had assignments from coast to coast, becoming Chief of the Washington AP Bureau and also an assistant general manager of The Associated Press.

In 1950, he was the elected President of The Associated Press — the first former employe to gain this post since the organization was founded in 1848.

Mr. Miller is president of the Gannett chain of 17 newspapers, three radio and two television stations in New York, Connecticut, New Jersey, and Illinois. He also publishes two Rochester, New York, papers.

Mr. Miller credits his parents with having set the mental patterns that led him to newspapering. His father was a clergyman who, Mr. Miller says, "encouraged me to a sustained interest in current events." His mother read to the family every night.

Before he left AP as Washington bureau chief to join the Gannett Newspapers in 1947, Mr. Miller got to know on close terms Presidents Roosevelt and Truman, Generals Marshall and Eisenhower, and other highly-placed officials. His contacts often produced information that could not be published at that time. It was invaluable, however, for background. In 1946 — long before the majority of Americans were aware of the situation — Mr. Miller wrote: "Russia constitutes a greater threat to the American way of life than Hitler did at the start of his aggression."

In addition to various posts he holds in professional and press organizations, Mr. Miller also is an active participant in national, community, and church layman affairs.

*But none of these things move me, neither
count I my life dear unto myself . . . .*

ACTS 20:24 *King James Version*

DR. J. EARL MORELAND

President, Randolph-Macon College

MY FAVORITE TEXT first came forcefully to my attention when I heard a sermon during student days at Southern Methodist University in 1917 by Dr. Clovis G. Chappell, Minister of Highland Park Methodist Church, Dallas, Texas. Dr. Chappell stressed the fact that selflessness and self-giving are the keys to success in the Christian enterprise.

This verse served well during World War I when I was trying to qualify for service in the infantry division of the Colonel Randolph Battalion, in Washington, D. C.

It served in good stead during two years of post-graduate study at Southern Methodist University when I was seeking to complete my post-graduate degree and prepare for service in South America. It was an invaluable aid in writing a master's thesis. It conduced to finding the time, the energy, the concentration, and the effort necessary for the completion of post-graduate work.

The truths stated in this text were proven many, many times during 14 years of residence and labors in South America. As those truths were proven through experiment, a sincere, sustained effort was made to emphasize their validity and value to hundreds of students at Porto Alegre College in Porto Alegre, Brazil.

The verse continued to serve as support and inspiration during four years of service at Scarritt College. Students in that senior college and graduate school were preparing themselves for service in many parts of the world. They were very often in need of counsel, and the counseling was made available not only to the students who were preparing for missionary service but, as well, to those who were returning after long years of service in China, India, Korea, Japan, Latin America, and Africa. It seemed to provide strength and inspiration.

Finally, during the past 24 years at Randolph-Macon College, it has been my privilege to seek to emphasize the truths represented by and emphasized in the text to students at this college. Particularly has the text been valuable in these more recent years following the termination of World War II when students are beset with a multitude of problems, doubts, perplexities, and difficulties. I believe it is no exaggeration to say that the truths of that statement by St. Paul have served as a source of strength, of renewed confidence, and of inspiration to hundreds of students at Randolph-Macon as they have sought to put them to the test in their own lives.

I dare to believe that it would be difficult, if not indeed impossible, to overstate the value of St. Paul's great affirmation for millions of men in many parts of the world.

→≫ ≪←

J. EARL MORELAND, the President of Randolph-Macon College in Virginia, is an outstanding and active Methodist lay leader.

The one-time educational missionary to Brazil was instrumental in the founding in that country of Porto Alegre College, of which he served as President from 1927 to 1934.

Dr. Moreland, a native of Texas, returned to the United States to become Vice President of Scarrit College in Tennessee. Since 1939, he has been President of Randolph-Macon.

The lay leader, missionary, teacher, and college president is known for his patience, modesty, and "complete dedication."

In 1962, he received the "St. George Award" for "distinguished service to The Methodist Church." The presentation was made in Philadelphia on the 195th anniversary of the organization of St. George's Church, the world's oldest Methodist church in continuous service.

In addition to participation in various educational activities on a regional and national scale, the educator's services also have been employed in areas not always associated with a teacher. For example, he is a member of the board of directors for a bank in his community and is a member of the Ashland Planning Commission.

His many civic interests and activities range over a varied group of organizations primarily concerned with the "education" of people so that they will understand each other and learn to live together harmoniously.

Dr. Moreland has been a Central Committee member of the World Council of Churches and has attended as a delegate all sessions of that ecumenical body in this country and abroad. He was a member of the 1958 organizational assembly of the National Council of Churches and has been a board member since that time.

Love ye therefore the stranger; for ye were strangers in the land of Egypt.

DEUTERONOMY 10:19 *Jewish Publication Society Version*

RABBI ISRAEL MOWSHOWITZ

President, New York Board of Rabbis

THIS VERSE in the Bible has helped mold my entire philosophy of life and has been an inspiration to me throughout the years.

Human nature is so constituted that we tend to dislike the unlike. The fear and distrust of the stranger, or xenophobia, are rather wide-spread in all cultures. Even the enlightened Greeks would speak of all strangers as barbarians.

The Sages of the Talmud point out that 36 times does the Torah admonish us not to oppress or mistreat the stranger. The Torah bids us to love him as a fellow human being and enjoins us to have one law, "To him that is homeborn, and unto the stranger that sojourneth among you."

When we learn to overcome the dislike of the unlike, we become more nearly human. When we fulfill the Biblical injunction to love not only the member of the same family, or the same tribe, or the same religion, but even him who is alien to us and a stranger, we then discover the idea of humanity.

Montaigne, in one of his essays, observes that "Nature has placed us in the world free and unbound; we imprison ourselves in certain narrow districts, like the Kings of Persia, who bound themselves never to drink any water other than that of the River Choaspes, foolishly renouncing their right of using any other waters, and dried up, so far as they were concerned, all the rest of the world." The love of the stranger opens up to us new worlds of friendship and understanding. By embracing the stranger, we enrich our own lives, and broaden the horizons of our own living.

There is also another level of interpretation of this meaningful verse. In a very real sense, each one of us is a stranger and suffers from a sense of isolation, alienation and loneliness. It requires much wisdom and maturity to develop a sense of belonging, to feel at home in the world. We are all strangers in the land of Egypt, in all kinds of Egypts, some imposed upon us from the outside, and some self-imposed. There are the enslavements of fear and insecurity, of self-centeredness and narrow-mindedness, of poverty and disease, and many others too numerous to mention. Who knows what it is that may trouble our fellowman's heart and make him an alien, a stranger in our midst? Who knows what it is that severs the lines of com-

[168]

munication betwen our neighbor and ourselves and makes him who lives next door to us and who seems to be so very much like us, a stranger nevertheless?

I know the burden that I carry; should I not, therefore, sympathize with every human being who, like me, has his own burden to carry? I know what troubles my heart and what makes me sometimes feel like a stranger and suffer from a sense of alienation; I should, therefore, learn to love every stranger and learn to respect the tear in the soul of every human being, embracing all men as brothers.

⇛ ⇜

ISRAEL MOWSHOWITZ, the tall, boyish, and buoyant spiritual leader of the Flushing, N. Y., Hillcrest Jewish Center, which is named for him and where he has life-time tenure, is a many-sided man.

Rabbi Mowshowitz is a religious scholar, licensed psychologist, university instructor, and a distinguished contributor to the promotion of interracial understanding. He was the associate director of the pioneering "Crossroads Africa" project that was a forerunner of the Peace Corps.

His wit and wisdom have made him a favorite with audiences wherever he speaks. He also can bring tears — as when in 1956 he conducted prayers in a Leningrad synagogue. One thousand fellow Jews were moved to tears.

One month after he arrived in Flushing in 1949 (from assignments as a Durham, N. C., spiritual leader and as a university teacher in Omaha), he started to work on the new center that today has a congregation of 1,800 member families. It is the largest Jewish Center on Long Island and one of the biggest in the nation.

His congregation, through the well-equipped Center, provides among other services a daily haven to a group of emotionally-disturbed children who are cared for by the Lifeline organization.

The Polish-born son of a rabbi, as President of the New York Board of Rabbis, heads an organization of some 800 Orthodox, Conservative, and Reformed clergymen

Whoever forces thee to go for one mile, go with him two.

MATTHEW 5:41 *Confraternity Version*

FR. JOHN O'BRIEN

Research Professor of Theology, The University of Notre Dame

FOR MORE THAN 50 YEARS these words of Our Lord have echoed and re-echoed in my memory. At first they startled me, then gripped me with their haunting challenge and command. They go to the heart of the Gospel and illustrate the principle central in Christ's ethical teaching: "Overcome evil with good."

[171]

This counsel of perfection has had hard sledding over the centuries because it runs against the grain of human nature, which demands an eye for an eye and a tooth for a tooth. Yet it constitutes the test of Christ's discipleship: the willingness to return good for evil and love for hatred. It mirrors an unshakeable faith in the invincible power of goodness, unselfishness, self-sacrifice, magnanimity, and a generosity that seeks no repayment here below.

At first glance this precept, like its companions — turning the other cheek and loving your enemies — appears utterly impractical. Paradoxical as it may seem, however, its fulfillment pays rich dividends in peace of mind and happiness, while the person who meets insult or injury with revenge finds the evil multiplied a hundredfold. It is a segment of that larger paradox with which Christ also startled His hearers, "He who loses his life for my sake, will find it."

The effort to translate Christ's command into daily conduct, to do more than is required by strict justice, to return good for evil, and to walk the second mile in surplus service transforms one's whole life. This is illustrated in the life of Booker T. Washington, the founder of Tuskegee Institute.

Daily discrimination, social ostracism, and scowling prejudice tempted him fiercely to strike back. But he rose above the instincts of our fallen nature and said: "No man, either white or black, from North or from South, shall drag me down so low as to make me hate him." When he died in 1915, Andrew Carnegie thus voiced the sentiment of millions: "History will tell us of two Washingtons, one white, one black, both fathers of their people."

The effort to put the counsel of Jesus into daily practice transformed Toyohiko Kagawa into one of the noblest ethical leaders of Japan. When confronted by a bully who demanded his few coins to buy liquor, Kagawa refused. Whereupon the ruffian rained blow after blow upon his face, knocking out several of his teeth and causing blood to stream from his lips.

But Kagawa did not strike back. His vision of Jesus, buffeted, spat upon and saying, "If someone strike thee on the right cheek, turn to him the other also," restrained him. Terror-stricken, the brute fled in dismay.

There is something deep in the heart of man that crumples at the sight of a person who innocent, defenseless, and unafraid bears the blows heaped upon him without striking back. Physical force falls on its knees in awe when confronted with the moral might of a love that walks the second mile in surplus service. Each day I pray, "God, give me the grace to walk that second mile."

-))) (((-

JOHN A. O'BRIEN, research professor of theology at the University of Notre Dame, received his Ph.D. degree from the University of Illinois where he established the Newman Foundation, consisting of residence halls, chapel, and social center for Roman Catholic students, the largest in the United States.

For some 20 years, he conducted accredited courses in the philosophy of religion for University of Illinois students of all faiths. While serving as Director of the Newman Foundation, he received a gold Knights of Columbus pin from the Acacia Fraternity (an organization composed exclusively of Protestants) in appreciation of his influence for friendship and goodwill among students of all faiths on the campus.

Dr. O'Brien has lectured at many of the leading universities in this country and in England. He is the author of some 15 books in the fields of philosophy, religion, and education. Some of these have been translated into many foreign languages and have achieved wide circulation. Among the best known of his works is *Truths Men Live By,* which has been acclaimed as a classic by leaders of all faiths.

He is a contributor to various national magazines and other publications and writes occasional features for newspaper syndicates. He holds a Testimonial Letter of Gratitude from the St. Joseph County (Indiana) Ministerial Association for his action in defending Protestant ministers against sweeping charges of Communism that were made in the 1950s.

[173]

Render therefore unto Caesar the things
which are Caesar's and unto God
the things that are God's

Matthew 22:21 *King James Version*

JAMES CASH PENNEY

Founder, J. C. Penney Company, Inc.

As a business man, I think of these Bible words as applying directly to the great truth that there can be no arbitrary line drawn between the secular and the sacred even though we are directed to "render unto Caesar the things that belong to Caesar and unto God the things that belong to God."

In other words, I believe the Great Teacher was admonishing men to do their duty and their whole duty; that even though those who came to Him obeyed all the laws of their faith they failed to pay their taxes and thus could not hope to be free from condemnation.

Just as certainly He meant that taxpayers, however respected by their business associates, had not done their full duty until they had returned proper thanks and service to their Creator.

The man who does not give to business what honest business deserves — his best — is failing in his duty. He may succeed in a measure; but his success is always less than it might have been and is of a kind that will disappear under pressure.

My father was both a clergyman and a business man. One of the things about him that impressed me was that to him there was no difference between the farm and the church when it came to the matter of faithfulness. He did his best on the farm, in the details of his daily living, and in his relationships with his fellow men; and he was devoted and consecrated in his religious service.

If it is possible to live the Christian life at any point it should be possible to live it in *all* relationships of one's life. A man should first ask himself, when he faces a question of business choice, "Is this worthy of my best?" If the answer is "Yes," he should go into it, not only retaining his self-respect, but also holding fast to the highest Christian standards.

Some men attain positions of distinction in the business world and are entrusted with responsibilities involving the well-being of hundreds, or even thousands, of their fellow men, while others never get beyond the village store or the country office. But again and again I find those who are in positions often regarded as insignificant doing so much for the people of their communities that others in spectacular positions are shamed by comparison.

Why is this? Is it because these unknown people are

giving everything they have to their work; unselfishly counting their gains not by money profits but by the service they can render. These humbler members of society do not separate the secular from the sacred. They recognize them as united and in their own lives they are one.

The world at large never heard of my father but *I* know he was a successful man. I know he lived largely because he lived truly, because he rendered "unto Caesar the things which are Caesar" even as he rendered "unto God the things that are God's."

→»-«←

JAMES CASH PENNEY, the famed "Golden Rule Merchant" has been associated for threescore years with the firm he founded.

He was President of the J. C. Penney Company for 15 years, chairman of the board for 41 years, and, since 1958, he has been a director. The firm now has some 1,700 department stores.

When he was 19 years old, fresh off his preacher-father's farm, he became a clerk in a Hamilton, Missouri, store.

By the time he was 26, Mr. Penney was a partner in The Golden Rule Store of Kemmerer, Wyoming. By 1907, he had bought out the firm's three stores to launch the J. C. Penney Co. And by 1959, under his inspirational force and merchandising acumen, the department store chain that bore his name had become the fifth in size among all U. S. mercantile companies.

Many articles, pamphlets, and books have been written about the "Main Street Merchant" — all attesting his reliance on the simple faith instilled in him as a boy by his parents.

Nevertheless, in 1931 — when the fruits of a lifetime, including an estimated $40,000,000 fortune, had been wiped out by the depression — Mr. Penney considered himself a failure at the age of 56. He suffered a physical and nervous collapse, was a patient in a sanitarium, and as he has put it, "waited for the end."

Instead, the breakdown was what he has called the turning point of his life. And he attributes his complete recovery at that time to his finding his real self through daily prayer.

[177]

*I will not leave you comfortless: I will
come to you.*
JOHN 14:18 *King James Version*

*Who also hath made us able ministers of
the new testament; not of the letter,
but of the spirit: for the letter killeth,
but the spirit giveth life.*

II CORINTHIANS 3:6 *King James Version*

DR. DANIEL A. POLING

Chairman and Editor , Christian Herald Magazine

DIFFICULT IT IS, if not impossible, for me to give my favorite Bible words. The scripture that has enriched my life beyond all others is always associated with the particular occasion, and even as occasions are different so the passage for the occasion may be different.

[179]

On the first Friday of February, 1918, I stood in an English box respirator behind gas curtains in a dugout on the Toul front. Mustard gas was coming over in three-inch-high explosive shells. For 90 minutes, we were trapped and helpless. It was then that these words came to me from St. John 14:18: "I will not leave you comfortless: I will come to you." And He came. The promise was fulfilled. From having been completely possessed by fear I was completely reassured and calm.

Across the years from that dark morning until now, again and again that promise for me has been demonstrated and fulfilled. Surely for such a time as that, and again and again since, these are the words of my favorite scripture passage.

But there is another passage that has become just about my life text: II Corinthians 3:6, "Who also hath made us able ministers of the new testament; not of the letter, but of the spirit: for the letter killeth, but the spirit giveth life." That verse needs no homiletical teacher.

-》》》 《《《-

DANIEL A. POLING, minister of religion, editor, novelist, radio speaker, civic leader, counsellor of philanthropists and friend of youth, is a dynamic figure in American life.

For more than a quarter of a century, Dr. Poling has been an outstanding leader of the church and a special friend and counselor of youth. During this time, his influence has been felt throughout the world. He is the editor of *Christian Herald,* an influential and widely-circulated religious journal. He writes a syndicated column, "Americans All," that appears in leading daily journals. And he has a national radio broadcast every Sunday.

Dr. Poling is president of the World's Christian Endeavor Union and has traveled extensively in Europe; he has been around the world four times in connection with Christian Endeavor activities.

Dr. Poling is Chaplain of the Chapel of Four Chaplains in Philadelphia, an interfaith memorial to the four young clergymen of three faiths who lost their lives in the sinking of the *S.S. Dorchester*. His son, the Reverend Clark V. Poling, was one of those chaplains. The tradition of the ministry was strong in the family; Dr. Poling's own father was also a minister.

The first clergyman to receive the Medal of Merit, highest civilian award given by the United States Government, Dr. Poling holds many public honors, including citations from the American Legion, B'nai B'rith and the American Federation of Labor.

*You shall love the Lord your God with all
your heart, and with all your soul,
and with all your mind.
You shall love your neighbor as yourself.
On these two commandments depend all the
law and the prophets.*

MATTHEW 22:37, 30, 40 *Revised Standard Version*

DR. MILLER A. F. RITCHIE

President, Pacific University

IN COMMON with countless other non-theologians I gain most inspiration from those scriptural passages that seem to relate directly to the practical daily relationships of people.

For me the Great Commandment in Matthew is the most soul-searching piece of scripture: "You shall love the Lord your God with all your heart, and with all your soul, and with all your mind. . . . You shall love your neighbor as yourself. On these two Commandments depend all the law and the prophets."

The part of this quotation that is not often used is the last line. To those of us who become either confused or impatient with the endless ramifications of creeds and theological analyses, this footnote to Christ's admonition is very reassuring.

It says to us that the essence of Christian faith is the translating of the principle of love into every dimension of our lives. All too often this principle of love is expressed in a soft, namby-pamby sort of attitude. Too often it is limited to words and safely innocuous acts and may even be a defensive screen behind which people sometimes hide to avoid the difficult and the unpopular.

I have always felt that there is a kinship between the quotation from the Master and the words of one of his biblical forerunners, the Prophet Amos, whose theme was "justice." His words are unforgettable:

> *"Hate evil, and love good, and establish*
> *justice in the gate;*
> *it may be that the Lord, the God of hosts,*
> *will be gracious to the remnant of Joseph."*

> *"Take away from me the noise of your songs;*
> *to the melody of your harps I will not listen.*
> *But let justice roll down like waters, and*
> *righteousness like an everflowing stream."*
>
> AMOS 5:15, 23, 24

We do not love our fellowmen very much unless we are willing to demand equal justice for all of them. Our Christian love is indeed soft if it is reserved only for those of our own kind and of our own views. Our protestations of concern for youth are weak unless we are willing to see that opportunity is available to every boy and girl for an education to develop his potential for himself, his family, his country, and mankind.

[184]

The intervening centuries have not dimmed the pertinence of Christ's call to *love* and Amos' call to *justice*. They speak to us today with greater urgency than ever.

-》》-《《-

DR. MILLER A. F. RITCHIE, who strongly believes in education and human relations, has been President of Pacific University in picturesque Forest Grove, Oregon, since 1959.

The educator, who is a native of Virginia, won national recognition as chairman of the University of Miami's department of human relations.

An articulate man with a deep understanding of the needs of people and the patience of a teacher, Dr. Ritchie is much in demand as a lecturer before national and regional groups.

The World War II Naval officer has been a public school teacher, supervisor, college professor, and administrator.

He is the author of numerous articles in professional journals. And he has been given several citations for his contributions in the field of education and human relations.

Dr. Ritchie was President of Hartwick College in Oneonta, N. Y., prior to accepting the Presidency of Pacific University.

A devout man, Dr. Ritchie is widely respected throughout the Pacific Northwest for his own human relationships in dealing with people and for his efforts in behalf of education, the arts, and organizations such as the American Red Cross and the YMCA.

For God so loved the world, that he gave his only begotten Son, that whosoever believeth in him should not perish, but have everlasting life.

John 3:16 *King James Version*

DALE AND ROY ROGERS

WE BELIEVE THAT with all our hearts. We base our lives upon it. In 1948, we accepted the Lord Jesus Christ as our personal Saviour — and put our trust in Him. We asked Him to come into our hearts through His Holy Spirit, and make us anew — and use us for His Purpose in the world.

[187]

He changed our lives, gave us a fresh, new viewpoint — and gave us a chance to serve Him in many areas of our lives. We believe the only true happiness to be found is to be found in Him, who said "I am the way, the truth and the life."

It is hard to comprehend a love so great as the love of God. It staggers the imagination. Being parents of eight children, we cannot imagine how God could love a sinful, heedless world enough to send His Only Son down to save the world — through a life that was sinless, unappreciated and finally crucified on the Cross of Calvary.

We are old-fashioned Bible believers who believe that Jesus Christ was born of a virgin, lived a perfect life, died and rose bodily from the grave to conquer death for those who put their trust in Him. We believe that He will return to this earth, just as the Bible says — and take His followers unto Himself for eternity.

This is why we love Him so. He has given us true security and a reason for living the best we know how — by His Grace.

-》》-《《-

DALE AND ROY ROGERS, the "King and Queen of the Cowboys" credit the public for their success on the screen, television, and in traveling show productions.

As a result they have given freely of their time to charities and citizenship service in many fields. Roy and Dale have been given awards and citations for their humanitarian services, "Americanism," morale work during World War II, "clean and wholesome entertainment," and "effective leadership to the homeless and orphaned children and to the mentally retarded."

During his career, Roy has starred in 86 feature motion pictures that are still playing all over the world and being rerun on television. So widespread is his popularity for his Westerns that once in Africa for a safari he was mobbed by autograph fans in out-of-the-way towns he had never heard of. And just before Christmas 1961, while in South America to visit cities where he distributed toys to poor children, some 300,000 people turned out to see him in Lima, Peru.

The hour-long specials in which Roy and Dale are starred draw an estimated 35,000,000 television viewers. And the husband-wife team are seen by additional thousands at rodeos and other exhibitions where they appear in an eight-act traveling show.

Roy rode to fame across the movie rangeland with a gifted golden palomino, Trigger. Equally beloved by his fans today is a similarly-gifted horse, Trigger, Jr. The first Trigger turned 30 years old in 1963.

Both Dale and Roy are devout Christians who "speak up" on spiritual matters when they feel they should. Once during a show they were doing at a Houston rodeo, Roy held up his hand for attention at the completion of one of his songs and indicated he had something he wanted to say.

He told the huge crowd about the mail he received from children and how they frequently asked him didn't he think it was sissy for them to go to Sunday school. "I want to say right here and now that it isn't sissy at all," the King of Cowboys said. "In fact, I think that going to Sunday school is one of the best things any child can do."

It is the same young people who see him on the motion and television screens, who watch him in person, and who write him for advice who, Roy says, are the secret of his success. "If they didn't like me and I didn't like them, I'd be nowhere in show business."

*And so he that had received five talents
came and brought other five talents,
saying, Lord thou deliveredst unto me
five talents; behold I have gained
beside them five talents more. His
Lord said unto him, well done, thou
good and faithful servant: thou hast
been faithful over a few things, I will
make thee ruler over many things:
enter thou into the joy of thy Lord.*
MATTHEW 25:20-21, *King James Version*

GOVERNOR TERRY SANFORD

Governor of North Carolina

THE BIBLICAL INJUNCTION (MATTHEW 25:14-30) to use our talents rather than burying them is one that means much to those working in the public service. It has always seemed to me that this parable of the talents applied especially to Americans and particularly to those in government.

America was founded by people who were willing to invest their talents, to run the risk of a mysterious ocean and to move to a land about which little was known in order to plant new crops in new fields.

Those first Americans, who came to the coast of North Carolina under Sir Walter Raleigh's direction, may have lost a colony but they found a nation. In later years, Americans such as Daniel Boone, who pushed across the Appalachians, and others in New York and Pennsylvania and Kentucky who pushed from the mountains into the great plains of the Middle West, and still later, those who followed the paths of wild animals to the West Coast were following the advice of this parable.

We have, in this nation, long since discarded the notion that public service was merely something to tolerate, a necessary evil to contend with. We have decided that government can be a dynamic force for good, doing those things which the people of the nation, and of the State, and of the community collectively wish to do.

We have pooled and we have invested our talents to build schools, roads, ports, hospitals, and universities.

It is the same in our free enterprise system. There are many examples of companies that "buried their talents," that retrenched after World War II out of fear of a depression, that were afraid to invest in the future because they saw in the future only a bleak picture. Other companies invested heavily and have profited from that investment.

In the lives of individual citizens, you can see the story of the talents told and retold in our nation. There are those who invest their talents and who despite any handicaps of birth or of physical infirmity, turn toward the future. It is these people — who dared to overcome their handicaps, who dare to blaze new trails — who have made our nation strong.

In a world that is throwing off old shackles and building new nations, I believe the parable of the talents can be put to good use.

TERRY SANFORD, the Governor of "The Old North State" is an exciting personality and a man of strong convictions with an abiding interest in education.

The North Carolinian credits his retired schoolteacher mother with having exerted a profound influence on him, and he has made "quality education" an obtainable goal for all boys and girls in his own state as well as in the entire South.

Elected to office in 1960, Governor Sanford is the first Southern Governor to call for employment by both private and governmental agencies without regard to race, color, or creed.

During his first two years of office, the State General Assembly approved the greatest increase in support for public school children of any state in the nation. And in the same two years, approximately half-a-billion dollars in new industrial plants were built in North Carolina.

The Governor is a boyish-looking fellow, casually informal, and unpretentious. He is described as being an excellent organizer and administrator and as an ambitious and skilled politician.

As a boy, Terry Sanford, according to his mother, was "a mischievous, beguiling little boy who loved to play tricks on the family." He still has a penchant for humor.

He received his law degree from the University of North Carolina, fought in World War II, practiced law, and served as a State Senator before becoming the Tar Heel State's ninety-third Governor.

He is active in Methodist affairs and has served that denomination as a district lay leader and as board chairman of North Carolina's Methodist College. He has held a variety of civic offices and has participated in political deliberations from Raleigh to Los Angeles.

Fellow Governors from 16 other Southern states have accorded the Governor the unusual honor of electing him twice as chairman of the Southern Regional Education Board that is supported by a compact of states.

[193]

Whatsoever thy hand findeth to do, do it
with thy might; for there is no work,
nor device, nor knowledge, nor wisdom,
in the grave, whither thou goest.

ECCLESIASTES 9:10 *King James Version*

GENERAL ROBERT LEE SCOTT, Jr.

Brigadier General, USAF (Ret.)

MY DAD GAVE ME the first hint that eager as I was my enthusiasm might need be curbed. It was during the period when I "hacked" freight trains — not so much to travel as to win my letter in the Hobo Club. I had to accrue at least 10,000 miles.

For a time I must have improved for I know I wanted to win Dad's favor. I turned to moth collecting. Just as

[195]

I had to accumulate thousands of miles aboard the freights, I couldn't be content with a dozen or so species. I had to go all-out on anything I ever did. I took those moths by the thousands too.

I got the aviation bug next. But while the average boy is content to build model planes, I built mine life-size similar to the Wright Brothers glider. And though there were no Kitty Hawk sand dunes in Macon, I got my glider to the top of a building, ran down the sloping roof, flew out over a magnolia tree to my first flight and my first and only crash. After that, I went 6,000,000 miles and spent three and a half years in actual flight. But that's getting ahead of my story and my favorite Bible verse.

By the time I won my wings at Kelly Field and became a real Army Air Corps pilot, I not only felt sorry for people who weren't so fortunate as to fly, but I even felt sorry for a good many pilots. They could fly, but I realized they didn't live for it. From that moment on I strove to be not the oldest, as the old addage was then, but the boldest and thus — in my opinion — the best. I vowed to be ready to fit into the niche that fate had for me.

Pearl Harbor came and brought World War II to me along, I was positive, with my niche. And though those critics had been right about my being technically past fighter-pilot age — I managed regardless. By that time I'd flown so much, silly years alone didn't count. Mine was a second nature, I flew as a reflex, maybe as an addict — but I was ready.

Oh, I don't mean I won the war — not even the little bush league one in which I fought. But I did win-out being there, in spite of the trace of gray at my temples and after cold statistics had done its best to close the door on me. I closed the cockpit canopy on my fighter plane and served out my destiny, led hundreds of missions, shot down some enemy bombers who were trying to get me — and ultimately sort of fell into the best job in my war — commanding and leading the Flying Tigers under General

Chennault in China. That wasn't all — I got to be a general myself, in the Pentagon, and even got out of there healthy and still wanting to fly.

Until now, a good many years and more and more miles later, still not satisfied that I've seen enough across the horizons, still with the days not long enough, I think the explanation to all my dreams lies in ECCLESIASTES 9:10.

"Whatsoever thy hand findeth to do, do it with thy might; for there is no work, nor device, nor knowledge, nor wisdom, in the grave, whither thou goest."

-»» ««-

ROBERT LEE SCOTT, JR., in retirement, retains his enthusiastic zest for life, his interest in doing things, and his early-developed ability to describe and record his exploits and aspirations.

As a lecturer and author, the Georgia-born veteran aviator provides many who come within his orbit with inspiration and enthusiasm for doing well the tasks that are set before them.

As a matter of fact, the famed pilot, if he could have his way, would probably still be up in the "wild, blue yonder" winging his way to new adventures and added glory.

But being grounded by the technicalities of age has not diminished General Scott's relish for life nor his desire to conquer new horizons.

The Eagle Scout, who scaled mountains as a boy because they were there, climbed his way to professional attainment in the early days of flying to become a fighter pilot, the commander of World War II's famed Flying Tigers, and ultimately the peak when he was made an Air Force general.

He has recorded much of the drama, the satisfactions that come from having served one's country in times of peace and war, and his personal ethos in such popular books as *God Is My Co-Pilot, Chennault of China,* and *Boring a Hole in the Sky.*

General Scott maintains headquarters in Phoenix, Arizona, from which he flies — naturally — to his various platform assignments. He admits to still having what he describes as a "flying fixation."

My peace I give to you

JOHN 14:27 *Revised Standard Version*

LOUIS B. SELTZER

Editor, The Cleveland Press

BY THE GRACE OF A FATHER who himself believed profoundly in the Bible, I read it as a small boy five times before emerging from my teens.

Into the very fiber of my being, into the farthest recesses of my conscious and subconscious mind; into the continuing, unceasing unfolding of life, its problems, its joys, its sorrows, its unhappinesses, its challenges, its inevitable crosses and unexpected blows, its adversities, its high plateaus — into all of these, as a consequence of my total absorption of the Bible into my heart and mind, has come the strength of His teachings and His own examples.

Of all that the Bible taught, of all the infinite counsel, wisdom, inspiration, strength, the one facet that stands out pre-eminently, the one guiding light, the one refuge and sanctuary in time of stress and strain, travail and torment is that which I quote above, and again, here:

"My peace I give to you . . ."

From Him who gave all, who suffered indignity, humiliation, physical and inner suffering, and, who, therefore, from a life of understanding beyond that which any of us ever experiences, He gave to us the most precious gift within His power — if we but take it as He intended it, the Peace that itself passeth understanding.

⇢⤛

LOUIS B. SELTZER, editor of *The Cleveland Press* believes that an editor's place is in the mainstream of his community — not in an ivory tower. That's why he spends more time bustling about his native city, maintaining personal contacts and friendships that include bootblacks and bank presidents, than he does warming a chair in his "front office."

The Seltzer formula for producing a successful newspaper — and *The Press* has become Ohio's largest daily newspaper during his 35 years as editor — is to maintain close and constant contact with every group and phase of the community it serves.

Mr. Seltzer's journalistic creed is summed up by the motto of his own paper, "The newspaper that serves its readers," and the motto of the Scripps-Howard Newspapers, which developed from *The Press*, "Give light and the people will find their own way."

The Cleveland editor pioneered in expanding newspaper coverage to include such fields as science, education, industry, medicine, welfare activities, and the "good deeds" of real people as well as crime and violence. Mr. Seltzer believes that newspapers must keep alert to the needs of their communities and constantly change with the times to keep readers abreast of local, national, and global developments that affect their daily lives.

The editor-to-be started his journalistic career as an office boy. He covered all beats as a reporter and was an editorial writer, political editor, city editor, and news editor before being appointed to the top job at *The Cleveland Press* in 1928.

Mr. Seltzer is an active member of many civic and professional organizations and has been elected to high office by various national groups.

For God so loved the world that he gave his
only Son, that whoever believes in
him should not perish but have
eternal life.

JOHN 3:16 *Revised Standard Version*

DR. RALPH W. SOCKMAN

Minister Emeritus Christ Church Methodist, New York, N. Y.

DURING MY EARLY MINISTRY in my New York parish there
were two devout members who were superintending the
McAuley Water Street Mission, located under Brooklyn
Bridge. They were the Reverend and Mrs. Alexander L.
Jones.

Mr. Jones wore on his lapel a little silver button bearing the number 316. He told me its scriptural origin and said that to him embodied the essence of the saving gospel. As I studied his life and work, I began to realize the reasons for his conviction.

Mr. Jones himself had been transformed from a life of dereliction to devoted Christian service. Each night in his mission he saw two sections of listeners. On one side of the aisle were the "down-and-outs" who had drifted into the meeting to get a bite to eat and a night's lodging. On the other side of the aisle was a company of men, clean, clear-eyed, well dressed, who had been converted. To see their faces and hear their testimony was an inspiration which I shall never forget and which is lacking in our comfortable conventional churches.

We church members are so prone to be concerned with secondary aspects of our religion. John 3:16 calls us back to the central and primary fact of our faith, which is God's love. It also describes divine love at its deepest, the sacrifice of a Son.

And the verse gives hope. It could, of course, convey to the self-centered person merely the hope of escaping eternal damnation. But when we repeat it in the light of Christ's concept of eternal life, we feel its promise of life here and now and not merely hereafter.

Thus John 3:16 not only expresses the heart of our gospel, but also the summation of it. In it abide "faith, hope, love, these three, and the greatest of these is love."

⟫⟩⟨⟪

RALPH W. SOCKMAN, often called the "Dean of the American Protestant Pulpit", survived the changes and struggles of America's most difficult religious field to break all known records of pulpit tenure in his first and only parish — New York City's Christ Methodist Church. In 1961 he completed a 45-year ministry in this pulpit.

Twenty-five-year-old Ralph Sockman took over the pastorate in 1916, after serving as associate minister for five years. The appointment was criticized because of his youth and inexperience. Nonetheless, he became one of the "foremost clergymen of all denominations in the United States."

Dr. Sockman, a vigorous young man who was restless by nature, harnessed his boundless energy into a moving religious and intellectual force toward a greater understanding between nations, races, and cultures. As a result, during his half-century of association with the Park Avenue church both Dr. Sockman and the church became internationally famous.

Dr. Sockman is still known as the man who led nine lives: as pastor, religious leader, builder, educator, author, radio-television personality, speaker, director of the Hall of Fame, and world traveler.

The recipient of honorary degrees from 21 outstanding colleges and universities, Dr. Sockman is himself a trustee of four universities. He also teaches at two seminaries, and has written some 20 books in addition to writing a popular syndicated newspaper column.

For 34 years Dr. Sockman ministered to millions over the Sunday morning "National Radio Pulpit" heard coast-to-coast in the United States and Canada, and has lectured in almost every major country in the world.

On three occasions, Dr. Sockman declined the opportunity of becoming a Bishop of the Methodist Church, electing to remain with his church that, despite the 1929 stock market crash, the depression and the war, grew until eventually in 1933 a new $3,000,000 church building was dedicated.

In his dark pinstripe suit and Homburg, Dr. Sockman has often been mistaken for a banker or a diplomat as he "moves with relaxed urbanity through a round of activity that would faze most captains of industry."

Upon his retirement in 1961 at the age of 70, Dr. Sockman had accepted world-wide lecture commitments that extended into 1965. When he speaks he starts with a problem — something that is likely to be troubling the men and women in his audience. Then Dr. Sockman goes back to the Bible for the solution, explaining: "Those answers have been valid for 1900 years."

*Thou shalt love thy neighbor as thyself:
I am the Lord.*

LEVITICUS 19:16 *Hebrew Bible*

LOUIS STEIN

President, Food Fair Stores

FAMILIARITY BREEDS LACK OF APPRECIATION, amongst other things. A close friend, an oft-quoted literary passage, a well-known work of art is usually taken for granted. Often this results in our failing to see the deeper meaning of the relationship. The famous verse from Leviticus, Chapter 19 of the Hebrew Bible, suffers from such over-familiarity. It is evoked as the basis for brotherhood, neighborliness and good will. This is correct. But there is a plethora of insights to be derived from this Biblical statement.

Love of neighbor, we are told, must be "as thyself." On first glance this call for self-love seems strange! Yet the truth is that proper self-respect and regard for one's own personality and being is a prerequisite for a proper relationship to one's fellow man. This does not mean self-centeredness or narcissism. It does not mean egotism and selfishness. It does teach, however, that the person who has no proper self-understanding and regard for his own dignity — a healthy self-love — cannot relate well to others.

One who hates himself, who is empty of purpose and inner strength, projects his own insecurities and unhappiness on others. The integrated person, with satisfying interests, goals in life and proper self-appreciation, has the capacity to love his neighbor. Self-depreciation and unnatural self-denial lead to the denigration of others as well.

The most difficult task is achieving the balance between self-love and "other-love." The context in which such balance can be achieved is suggested in the last part of the Biblical verse — often forgotten — "I am the Lord." A consciousness of God and His attributes of love and justice creates the proper framework for balanced relationships in society. A blending of concern for God, neighbor and self is the way to peace and fellowship in a free society of responsible people.

The Hebrew Bible, a living influence in the life of those who study its contents, has been interpreted by Rabbis, teachers and laymen throughout the ages. Each generation finds new guidelines in its instruction. For me, Leviticus 19:16 has been particularly inspiring. These are but a few of the insights which make this one of my favorite Biblical passages.

LOUIS STEIN, who worked as a grocery boy in his father's Union City, N. J., store on a daily allowance of 25¢ a day, became one of the nation's leading financial experts.

As President of the Food Fair Stores, with headquarters in Philadelphia, Mr. Stein is no longer confined to a daily expenditure of "10¢ for the tubes and 15¢ for two hot dogs and milk."

Nevertheless, associates say the financier and supermarket organizer still "lives modestly."

Young Louis graduated from Fordham University Law School in 1926 two years too soon to take the bar examination. He later became general counsel for Food Fair Stores. In the mid-thirties he successfully raised the first supermarket stock issue for his firm by convincing Wall Street of the soundness of the venture at a time when supermarkets were of little interest to the financial center.

Mr. Stein advanced to various executive positions with his company, becoming President in 1953. He is the original organizer of Food Fair properties formed to develop shopping centers. And he was the force behind the reorganization of the West Coast Fox Markets as part of his company's empire.

Highly respected for his financial acumen, Mr. Stein is "always on the phone" taking the pulse of the great food chain he heads. He loves to read financial reports. But he's fun at parties, too, his friends say.

Mr. Stein practices the "brotherly love" appropriate for a Philadelphian by giving freely of his talents and services to many causes for the better of the community, the nation, and the world.

A strong advocate of education as a key to this country's strength, he has, as chairman of a citizen's committee, helped to raise millions of dollars for Quaker City public schools. He also heads a citizen's group actively interested in a community college for Philadelphia.

Many groups have honored Mr. Stein with awards for his leadership and volunteer services, including a State of Israel commendation, the 1959 Brotherhood Award, the Fordham University Law School alumni medal of achievement, and the American Cancer Society Humanitarian Award.

Weeping may endure for a night, but joy cometh in the morning.

PSALMS 30:5, *King James Version*

DR. JESSE WILLIAM STITT

Village Presbyterian Church

RABBI IRVING J. BLOCK

The Brotherhood Synagogue

WHEN RABBI BLOCK and I were asked to indicate our favorite Bible passage the rabbi came into my study and said, "I know which passage of scripture you have picked." And he was right. The thing that surprised me, however, was that he, too, expressed the desire to write upon the same passage as his favorite.

[211]

Briefly, this is why Psalms 30:5 has meant so much to me. When I was in my teens, I was asked to speak at an Easter Dawn Service before a very large group of young people who were members of the Christian Endeavor Society in Detroit. I had no idea what to say, and I went to my minister asking for help. His answer was, "I cannot write your speech for you, but I can give you a text that speaks vividly of the period of time from Good Friday until Easter morning. It is, "Weeping may endure for a night, but joy cometh in in the morning."

In my own personal life these words have brought me through untold experience of sorrow and concern. In my ministry I have shared these words with a multitude of those who have "walked through the valley of the shadow of death" and have longed for the sunrise of the dawn.

Rabbi Block will tell you now of this same verse in his own way.

Many times I have watched the faces of troubled and perplexed people as they shared life's problems with me. They seemed stunned when I said, "It may be for your good." "How can you say that, when I am pained and beside myself?" they retorted.

The truth is that many people fail to see that the challenges of life are opportunities for growth and maturity. We live in a world where the tempo of life is fast. Hurrying and scurrying, we have little time to see beyond the immediate. We feel pain and we want immediate relief; we have a decision to make and we want an immediate answer; we have a problem and we want an immediate solution. Nothing can wait — everything is short-range.

The truth of life is that, in ethics, everything must be measured by the long-range. The philosophy, as expressed by my religious teachers, namely, "This, too, is for our good and this, too, shall pass," has set things in the right perspective and has had for me a most quieting influencing. I have come to see that today's illness is tomorrow's cure; today's worry is tomorrow's ease.

The most beautiful way of expressing it is in the words of the Psalmist, "Weeping may endure for a night, but joy cometh in the morning."

‑⟫‑⟪‑

IRVING J. BLOCK and JESSE WILLIAM STITT not only believe in religious brotherhood, they live it. New York's colorful Greenwich Village knows them as the joint occupants of the same house of worship: on Friday nights, Saturdays, and the Jewish High Holy Days it is called the Brotherhood Synagogue; on Sundays and Christian holy days, it is the Village Presbyterian Church. Should both Jewish and Christian observances fall on the same day, schedules are arranged so that each congregation can have a separate service.

Between times, the facilities are shared jointly. The clergymen have their offices on the same floor. And a Brotherhood Council, composed of 10 members from each congregation, meets in the building to plan joint programs. In the building's basement is an off-Broadway theater (Greenwich Village Mews Playhouse) where Village writers and actors display their talents.

Although Dr. Stitt and Rabbi Block exchange pulpits now and then, there is no religious tie between the two congregations. Each worships in its own tradition. However, on Thanksgiving Day the two congregations have a joint service and offer up their thanks to God.

The Rabbi and Minister travel around the city and the country together preaching brotherly love to lay and religious groups. They once won $10,000 on a television quiz show with Dr. Stitt answering questions about Judaism and Rabbi Block answering those on Christianity.

In 1960, both men were invited by the Foreign Ministry of the Bonn Government to visit West Germany in order to study anti-Semitic outbreaks and to tell their story of brotherhood-in-action during a good-will tour of West German cities.

*Hear, O Israel: the Lord our God, the Lord
is one. And thou shalt love the Lord
thy God with all thy heart, and with
all thy soul, and with all thy might.
And these words, which I command
thee this day, shall be upon thy heart;
and thou shalt teach them diligently
unto thy children, and shalt talk
of them when thou sittest in thy house,
and when thou walkest by the way,
and when thou liest down, and when
thou risest up. And thou shalt bind
them for a sign upon thy hand, and they
shall be frontlets between thy eyes.
And thou shalt write them upon the
doorposts of thy house and upon
thy gates.*

DEUTERONOMY 6:4-9 *Jewish Publication Society Version*

ADMIRAL LEWIS L. STRAUSS

Former Chairman, Atomic Energy Commission

ONE OF MY FAVORITE BIBLE PASSAGES is that above. For more than 30 centuries, it has been copied in the Hebrew language and written directly upon or affixed to the doorposts of the homes of observant Jews.

It is recited in the Sabbath prayers and, as it follows

the Ten Commandments in Deutoronomy, it is both a familiar and a cherished guide.

The translation that I have used is the version published by the Jewish Publication Society of America in 1917. It was prepared by the distinguished Hebraist and scholar, Rabbi F. de Sola Mendes.

—⟫⟪—

LEWIS L. STRAUSS, a veteran public servant, has had wide experience in government, business, and banking.

As a boy in Virginia, the future Admiral was a salesman for his father's wholesale shoe concern. He rose from this early job in life to become a millionaire, a Wall Street investment broker, an adviser to Presidents, and a policy guide and consultant on problems of the atomic age.

Admiral Strauss (he was one of the first Naval Reservists to reach Flag Rank by successive promotions during World War II) began his public service in 1917 when he was secretary to Herbert Hoover, then Administrator for the food relief program in Belgium.

This work led him into the banking investment firm of Kuhn, Loeb & Company where he became a partner. He resigned his partnership to accept appointment by President Truman to the Atomic Energy Commission.

In 1958, President Eisenhower appointed him Secretary of Commerce. He left the Department of Commerce and Government employment after his confirmation failed by three votes.

Since then, Admiral Strauss has maintained an office in Washington and has written a best-seller, *Men and Decisions*. He also runs a 1,400-acre farm in Virginia where he raises purebred Aberdeen Angus cattle.

Known as a fighter for unpopular causes, Admiral Strauss is a highly articulate and determined administrator and adviser. He is widely known for his civic, philanthropic, and religious interests and has been honored by many organizations in these fields with high honors and elective offices.

He is particularly associated with the inception and development of President Eisenhower's Atoms for Peace Program, which was publicly inaugurated by the President in 1953 at the United Nations General Assembly.

Admiral Strauss holds some of the nation's highest decorations that include the Distinguished Service Medal, Legion of Merit with Gold Star, and the Medal of Freedom awarded him by President Eisenhower. He also has been honored by France and Belgium.

Thou shalt love thy neighbour as thyself.

LEVITICUS 19:18 *King James Version*

CHARLES P. TAFT

Attorney

"LOVE," LIKE SO MANY WORDS, has worn smooth and lost meaning. Even St. Paul had to give it content by his essay to the Corinthians.

"Love" was, in the Greek of the New Testament, an invented word. The Christians could not use "Eros," with all its implications of sex. Plato used Eros to mean the self-appreciation that leads a man to self-betterment, in the Horatio Alger tradition, by his own efforts. That concept was not Christian either, though it amusingly resembles what Tawney wrote about.

So the Christians invented a word for love in our Christian sense — Agape. It is Agape that is "long suffering," and "kind," to St. Paul.

But the idea still eludes us. When I was asked to join a Ladies Home Journal dialogue two years ago called "What Is Virtue," I had to think this out. Here is my interpretation of it.

Love of neighbor is affectionate, perceptive concern for him and all others.

"Affectionate" goes even for one you don't like, a kind of standing aside to see him and yourself, with a little amusement, and a feeling that perhaps it's just as well for you to have the old bum or this nasty annoyer around as a stimulant.

"Perceptive" is the most essential part. Love has to put you inside the other person, to feel his reactions, and understand why he acts as he does.

"Concern" is not assertive, but is unwilling to accept a condition the other suffers, without trying to do something about it.

But this "Love" can be soft and sentimental, so that a necessary addition to it is toughness, the endurance of fortitude of the Romans. Jesus in the Lord's Prayer was tough: No forgiveness of our trespasses except as we forgive. Our choices at a crisis may be limited; a decision either way, may hurt someone.

Love cannot be just quiescent. Often it must speak out. The Puritan conscience is something we need in organizations, and in the democratic process. Labor unions, trade associations, and civic organizations die of dry rot when members sit on their hands and don't speak up in the discussion, or worse, don't even come to meetings.

Yet this has a limit, too; the Puritan can be arrogant. Above all love must be humble, with a listening ear for the possibility that God may be speaking through some one else, some one unimportant, or annoying, or young, or boring. Some contribution may come to the common good from unexpected places.

Love as we think of it in my text is shown in the Good Samaritan or the father of the Prodigal Son. But we need it today, as we live in a time of change, and a time of organizations. Only love can keep us serene amid shattering upsets. Only Christian love can be the lubricant that makes our overwhelmingly organized world work smoothly.

–»» «««–

CHARLES P. TAFT, son of the twenty-seventh President and brother of the late Senator Robert A. Taft, is a distinguished statesman, lawyer, and churchman in his own right.

Mr. Taft is known as "a warm, friendly man with a bright and fresh outlook, and a fundamental faith in the American system of private enterprise."

His amazing energies have made him an outstanding leader in political science, business administration, community and civic affairs, the Protestant Episcopal Church, health and welfare activities, and in the crusade for better government.

A long-time member of City Council and Mayor of Cincinnati in 1956 and 1957, Mr. Taft is an important figure in Cincinnati's famous City Charter Committee, the most successful and long-lived municipal reform movement in U.S. history. *Fortune* magazine rated him in 1957 as one of the nine best mayors, and his city as one of the best governed, in the United States.

Among the many positions he has held are President of the Federal Council of Churches (the first layman ever honored), former President of the Committee for a National Trade Policy, and Director of Wartime Economic Affairs in the State Department.

The direction Charles Taft's life was to take was already evident during his student days at Yale: he graduated second in his class and was an outstanding all-around athlete. He graduated at the head of his class from Yale Law School.

*Bless the Lord, O my soul: and all that is
within me, bless his holy name.
Bless the Lord, O my soul, and forget not all
his benefits.*
PSALMS 103:1-2 *King James Version*

DR. GARDNER C. TAYLOR

Pastor, Concord Baptist Church of Christ

IT WAS ON A CHILL Saturday evening in the fall of 1954 that this passage came to have an indescribably rich meaning for me. Our church had burned to the ground two years before. The needs of the congregation and the community demanded the erection of a building that was slated to cost more than $1,200,000.00. And ours was a community composed primarily of people of low income. But we had no choice in the light of the needs of the teeming Bedford-Stuyvesant section of Brooklyn with its 300,000 people but to make the attempt.

Funds ran out and we were face to face with the bleak prospect of having to halt work on the half-finished structure. Obviously, the damage of such a step to the morale of the congregation would be incalculable. The dream of a great and adequate building for Bedford-Stuyvesant was under imminent threat of sudden and bitter collapse.

In this circumstance, I walked dejectedly that Saturday evening into my make-shift study in the old, dilapidated building that we were using temporarily. Among the letters was one which bore no return address. Finally, I opened it.

To my utter amazement, it contained a cashier's check for $1,000 and a little white sheet of paper with the words "Psalm 103:1-2" on it. Nothing else! I turned to the 103rd Psalm and read the words "Bless the Lord, O my soul; and all that is within me, bless his holy name. Bless the Lord, O my soul, and forget not all his benefits."

Those words spoke strangely and compellingly to my spirit. The next morning in worship I reported the incident and the anonymous gift of $1,000. The reaction was electric, a strange surge of power passed through the congregation. We were "air-borne" from that moment and went forward to complete the new Concord Buildings.

This gift accompanied by the same Biblical reference was to be repeated each year until the debt was completely retired, but that first gift, illumined by the passage, was God's gift of new life and new faith to a tired, almost defeated people.

Now whenever I read the passage a strange, strong calm passes through me.

GARDNER C. TAYLOR, the pastor since 1948 of the more-than-11,500-member Concord Baptist Church of Christ in Brooklyn is noted for his eloquence and relevancy as a preacher and as a platform speaker. He also is an organizer and a man of great creative talents with an amazing supply of energy that propels him into the public light as a respected spokesman against school, housing, and job segregation.

Dr. Taylor was the first Negro, the first Baptist, and the youngest person to be elected President of The Protestant Council of the City of New York, a cooperative body of 31 denominations.

A tall, husky, virile man with a twinkling smile, Dr. Taylor speaks and acts forthrightly whenever he finds racial or religious discrimination. In effect, he says to metropolitan New York, "Physician, heal thy self."

While he was a member of the Board of Education of the City of New York, Dr. Taylor was frequently in the news and was the subject of several speculative articles on his availability as a political candidate for state or national offices.

As pastor of a huge Brooklyn parish, Dr. Taylor is preacher, counselor, and leader. When the church building burned in 1952, he launched a campaign for a new building and enlargement of facilities. Less than four years later, he led the Concord congregation into the new $1,700,000 church and educational buildings.

His influence as a preacher has brought him many honors, including an Oberlin alumni citation. His prophetic messages have been delivered throughout the nation from pulpits, at college convocations, at civic rallies, and from the rostrums of such assemblies as the World Baptist Alliance, which he addressed in 1947 in Copenhagen and in 1955 in London's Westminster Hall.

Thus saith the Lord, Let not the wise man glory in his wisdom, neither let the mighty man glory in his might, let not the rich man glory in his riches: But let him that glorieth glory in this, that he understandeth and knoweth me, that I am the Lord which exercise loving kindness, judgment, and righteousness, in the earth; for in these things I delight, saith the Lord.

JEREMIAH, 9:23-24 *King James Version*

COMMISSIONER
EDWARD THOMPSON

Fire Commissioner, The City of New York

IN THE ADMINISTRATION of the welfare of almost 15,000
men who, in truth and in fact, are mankind's greatest ser-
vants here on earth, and who daily risk their lives for
strangers whom they know not, whose sex, state of wealth,
natural origin, and state of health is unknown to them,

I find that the caution of the Prophet Jeremiah is most inspiring.

Since firemen are faced with the wisest, the mightiest, and the richest of men — some of whom from time to time espouse these traits far beyond their relative values here on earth — I find complete satisfaction in the obedience of the Lord's wishes when he seeks from me and our men kindness, justice, and righteousness in our actions.

The Scripture convinces beyond any doubt that certainly the Lord is delighted with this type of conduct by the great men of this department; and with full realization and appreciation of that as a fact, we seek to serve the people of this city in every respect.

➤➤➤ ◄◄◄

ED THOMPSON, who became New York City's Fire Commissioner in 1961, got his first appointment to the Fire Department in 1936 when he was a senior in Brooklyn Law School. He had the highest written examination paper of 30,000 candidates. The following year he was admitted to practice law before the New York Bar.

Until he went into the Navy in 1944, he carried out specialized legal responsibilities for the Fire Department. While on service in the Pacific, he was appointed City Magistrate by Mayor LaGuardia and he took the oath of office in an unusual ceremony on the sea wall of Manila Bay, where he was stationed, on his thirty-second birthday. He assumed the bench in 1946 following his discharge from the Navy and in 1952 was appointed Associate Justice, Court of Special Sessions. In 1957 he was designated Acting Queens County Judge, which position he held until he became Fire Commissioner.

An outstanding and distinguished community leader, the Commissioner has received many citations and awards. He has been active on a high level for many years in the Boy Scouts of America, in Lutheran Church lay work, the St. George Association (he was the first president of the Fire Department's chapter and he was organizer and first president of the national body), The Salvation Army, Brooklyn College alumni association, and similar groups. For a quarter of a century he has been a Bible class teacher in his parish church. And he has addressed Protestant, Roman Catholic, and Jewish congregations throughout metropolitan New York. He also is active in numerous military, civic, and fraternal organizations.

As an avocation, Commissioner Thompson sings a baritone or second tenor lead at various Roman Catholic and Protestant church shows and minstrels, and for more than 10 years he has sung at the annual show of the Queens County Bar Association.

*In all thy ways acknowledge him
and he shall direct thy paths.*

PROVERBS 3:6 *King James Version*

MRS. J. FOUNT TILLMAN

President, Woman's Division of Christian Service
of the Board of Missions of The Methodist Church

MY FAVORITE TEXT was printed on a scroll which hung
on a wall in the home of my childhood. Once used in a
country Sunday school, it was finally left hanging like a
turn-over chart set permanently, it seemed, to one verse:
Proverbs 3:6: "In all thy ways acknowledge Him and He
shall direct thy paths."

[231]

Neighbors would come to the house in the evening from my father's country store. Mother played the organ for them to sing hymns. I sang as lustily as they, with my eyes fixed on the old scroll, and the words seemed to dance with the vibrations of the organ.

An impression must have registered deeply in my subconscious mind, for in times of joy, of sorrow, of testing, or of any notable experience in my life, this is the first response that comes, whether in praise, in comfort, in guidance, or just in assurance of faith in general.

It was in later life that I learned of an ancient rabbi quoting this verse as the first principle on which all the work and hope of Judaism might be considered to hinge. The writer who quoted the rabbi, Bar Kappara, added that this was true not just for Judaism, but as the spiritual basis for all humanity. (*Interpreter's Bible,* Vol. IV., pp. 799-800)

"In all thy ways" today includes the launching of Sputniks, of Telstars, and Space Ships. The glory of God fills the temple of multiple universes. "Acknowledgment" means increasing recognition of greater manifestations of His power. Man continues his search whether in messages from mechanical satellites orbiting the earth, mysteries of cloud-cloaked Venus, or inspiration from the Star of Bethlehem. "In all thy ways" is personal, signifying involvement — men and women, clergy and laity, Protestant, Catholic, and Jew.

Interestingly enough, as I have considered other favorite lines of Scripture, all of them seem to bear a relation to this, including Jesus' quotation as to "the first and greatest commandment," and the second — "like unto it": ". . . Love the Lord thy God . . . and thy neighbor as thyself." To acknowledge God is to glorify Him, and His directions lead us in paths of love and service among our fellowmen.

Bereavements, auto accidents, a heart operation and other difficult experiences in life have been met with strength in part due to faith engendered by dedicated parents, but symbolized for me in that verse of Scripture. It is a resource for one who would grow into maturity.

[232]

SADIE TILLMAN, who lives on a farm in Tennessee, heads one of the largest bodies of church women in the world. There are nearly 1,800,000 members in the Woman's Division of Christian Service of the Board of Missions of The Methodist Church, of which she is President.

When Mrs. Tillman became President in 1956, her little hometown church (one on a four-point circuit) proclaimed a "Sadie Tillman Day" celebration in her honor, serving an "on-the-grounds dinner." It was necessary for the Tennessee Highway Department to patrol the road to handle the cavalcade of cars.

A former school teacher and a one-time missionary to China, Mrs. Tillman travels extensively in this country, attending committee meetings and keeping speaking engagements. Her official trips have taken her to four other continents where she has attended World Methodist Council and World Council of Churches meetings and mission consultations in Oslo, New Delhi, South Africa, Latin America, London, and Paris.

She seems to be in the right place at the right time. A folksy, approachable woman, Mrs. Tillman may lose her purse, mislay her coat or briefcase (because of an interruption, which she never resents, to listen to personal problems) — and yet she is rarely late for an appointment. She presides calmly and with dispatch at meetings of 10,000 or more women in the annual assemblies of her organization.

It is this inner calm that perhaps keeps Mrs. Tillman able to meet the grueling demands of travel and work her unsalaried office requires. Few people know that a mitral valve operation and regular medication keep her heart going. Or perhaps it is a dedicated sense of mission, love for her fellowman, and understanding that give her heart.

*Then one of them, which was a lawyer,
    asked him a question, tempting him,
    and saying, Master, which is the great
    commandment in the law?
Jesus said unto him, Thou shalt love
    the Lord thy God with all thy heart,
    and with all thy soul, and with all
    thy mind.
This is the first and great commandment.
And the second is like unto it, Thou shalt
    love thy neighbor as thyself.
On these two commandments hang all the
    law and the prophets.*

MATTHEW 22:35-40 *King James Version*

JAMES F. TWOHY

Now I MUST NOT DISTORT my reaction to this scriptural passage by ascribing to it any over-simplification of meaning or pretense of spiritual enlightenment on my part. As we know, the variety of religious experience is quite literally without measure nowadays, ranging as it does from authentic lightning flashes of emotional inspiration to the confirmatory comfort of intellectual corroboration.

For me, the above passage, in all its all-sufficient simplicity, has for many years fulfilled the latter purpose. It has provided a sure test and touchstone of all my religious belief, a definitive statement both of the means and of the end of all spiritual search and striving, as well as an enduring structural design of Christianity by Christ Himself, within which we may confidently practice our faith and live out our lives on earth.

I chose the King James Version of the text I have quoted from St. Matthew for two sentimental reasons.

The first reason is a sincere ecumenical salute to an immortal religious classic; the second, because this particular text, and my reaction to it, so long antedates my new-found English version. My familiarity with the King James Version corresponds in time to my first discovery of this definition of Christianity by our Lord Himself.

→»» «««-

JAMES F. TWOHY, California industrialist and noted Catholic lay leader, has been prominent in business, civic, and philanthropic affairs on the West Coast for many years.

As president of Twohy Brothers Company, an engineering, construction, and finance organization, Mr. Twohy was active until 1935 in heavy industrial, railroad, and other construction throughout the Western states, Canada, and Mexico. The firm, which was established in 1880 by his father, suspended activity when Mr. Twohy accepted a position with the Federal Government.

Mr. Twohy gained nation-wide prominence as the Governor of the Federal Home Loan Bank System (1939-46) and as a member of the Loyalty Review Board and of the U. S. Civil Service Commission.

[236]

Decorated as a Knight of Malta, he is highly regarded for his work with the Roman Catholic Commission for Intellectual and Cultural Affairs.

Mr. Twohy is especially interested in building good will and understanding among America's religious groups. He has long served as a member of the national board of directors of the National Conference of Christians and Jews and was national Roman Catholic co-chairman of NCCJ from 1954 to 1960.

*The fear of the Lord is the beginning
   of wisdom...*
PSALMS 111:10, PROVERBS 9:10

*The fear of the Lord is the beginning
   of knowledge...*
PROVERBS 1:7 *King James Version*

MARK VAN DOREN

Professor of English, Columbia University

"THE FEAR OF THE LORD is the beginning of wisdom. The fear of the Lord is the beginning of knowledge." Whatever the difference between wisdom and knowledge, and whether it be great or small, these sentences contain in my view the basic message of the Bible.

It is a message which the modern world has almost completely forgotten, but that does not subtract from its truth. Rather it adds to it, for light is thrown then on what is the matter with the modern world.

Modern man has decided that he can know all he needs to know by contemplating himself, that he can be wise in the wilderness of his own ideas and desires. He has stopped believing that the truth is something outside of himself: so far outside as to be at last — also at first — the whole truth rather than his part of it. The Bible called it the Lord's truth, and said it was to be feared as well as loved.

The fear and the love of all the truth there is, and the faith that this exists even though we shall never know it perfectly — that was and is the beginning of wisdom.

—»» «««—

MARK VAN DOREN, Professor of English at Columbia University for more than forty years, has been described by former student Thomas Merton in *The Seven Storey Mountain* as "an excellent man who really loves what he has to teach and does not secretly detest all literature, and abhor poetry, while pretending to be a professor of it."

Thousands of people, who have never met Dr. Van Doren personally, have been fascinated by the many gracefully written volumes of poetry, biography, and criticism that have earned him world acclaim in addition to the 1940 Pulitzer Prize for his collected poems.

Slender, wiry, and strong featured, Van Doren has the look of a man who has lived close to nature. He has frequently appeared on radio's literary round table, "Invitation to Learning," since its inception.

Professor Van Doren is as admired for his teaching as for the work that emerges on the printed page. In the classroom he is said to be the most modest of men. As he himself has said, with customary poetic power and beauty, "The modesty of the true scholar is neither a gesture nor a joke. To him it is quite literally the case that a science of anything presupposes a vast ignorance concerning it: an ignorance, indeed, so vast that even its very nature may never be understood."

Students through the years have considered it a privilege to be able to spend 50 minutes every other day or so with Professor Van Doren, knowing well that he puts into effect his expressed belief that: "Any man gives forth more than he was taught; sometimes the truth comes easily, as if it said itself."

*And God spoke all these words, saying:
I am the Lord your God, who brought
you out of the land of Egypt, out of the
house of bondage. (Therefore) You
shall have no other gods before me.*

EXODUS 20:1-3 *Revised Standard Version*

DR. AND MRS.
THEODORE O. WEDEL

DR. WEDEL: *Warden Emeritus, College of Preachers, Washington Cathedral*

MRS. WEDEL: *Assistant General Secretary, National Council of Churches*

THESE ARE FAMILIAR WORDS, words that introduce the Ten Commandments. They mean a great deal to us because of what they reveal about the God of the Bible, the God in whom we believe. He is a holy and righteous God, and those who believe in Him must obey His Laws.

[243]

The Ten Commandments are well-known to everyone in the Judeo-Christian tradition. Some modern people find them a stumbling block to faith. How can one believe, they seem to say, in an arbitrary God who makes harsh demands on His people? Where is the God of love of whom Christianity speaks? Such people have perhaps never listened to the striking sentence that introduces the law. Often, indeed, in teaching the Commandments, it is omitted.

But this sentence reminds us that our God is a God who acts first. He loves us before He asks our love in return. In both the Old and the New Covenants our obedience is called forth by His mighty acts of love. In the Old Testament story He delivered His people from slavery in Egypt. Then, as our passage tells us, He reminds them of what He has done — "I am the one who brought you out of bondage." The word *therefore* does not appear in the text, but surely it is there in meaning. *Therefore,* thou shalt have no other God. It is almost as though God's love were pleading with us. "After what I have done for you, how could you choose any other god?"

Similarly in the New Testament, God performs His mighty act of redemption through Jesus Christ before man had done anything to deserve it. Only then does He ask for our response of love and obedience. Saint Paul, in proclaiming the Christian faith, makes frequent use of the word *therefore.* Several times in his Epistles he rehearses the story of the life, death and resurrection of Jesus Christ and then goes on to say, "Therefore, brethren —."

Ours is no remote, powerful deity demanding obedience through fear. Ours is a God who first loves us. He loves, He acts, He saves. Our obedience to His commandments is the joyous response of grateful children. Christian ethics is grateful penitence.

⟫ ⟪

DR. AND MRS. THEODORE O. WEDEL — or Cynthia and Ted as they are affectionately known to their many admirers —

enjoy a joint fame for their individual accomplishments that propelled both to high honors within The Protestant Episcopal Church and in other areas of Christian leadership.

Dr. Wedel is an honorary canon of Washington Cathedral and Warden-Emeritus of the College of Preachers, an institution devoted to post-ordination training of the clergy of the Episcopal Church. His retirement in 1960 brought him such accolades as "a man's man, a gentleman, a Christian priest, counselor, scholar, and gifted teacher." He is now a researcher and teacher.

Mrs. Wedel, who in 1962 became Assistant General Secretary of the National Council of Churches after a distinguished career as a professional Episcopal Church worker, has been described as an "irrepressibly gay and delightfully impertinent redhead."

The Wedel's were married in 1939 in the old New York headquarters building of their church where both worked in the Christian Education department. As Mrs. Wedel recalls it, "There was only a glass partition between us, and this proved to be fatal."

Their life together has been described as a love affair "carried on openly under the very eyes of the Church" and one that has even "survived their total incompatibility in the matter of punctuality." Louis W. Cassels, writing in *The Episcopalian,* has pointed out that "Ted has a hair-shirt compulsion to be on time and Cynthia is incorrigibly and unrepentingly late for everything."

Dr. Wedel is one of the most widely-beloved and highly-respected American Christians of this century. In addition to the impact he made on thousands of young clergymen attending the College of Preachers in Washington, Dr. Wedel served with scrupulous fairness when elected in 1952 to the Presidency of the Episcopal Church House of Deputies—the most distinguished post a priest or layman can hold in that Church.

Mrs. Wedel — through her writing, lecturing, and unique capacity to work with people both in her church and in interdenominational positions of authority — has enchanted all who get to know her with her famed wit, vitality, and ability.

Together they give eloquent witness as co-speakers for the modern ecumenical movement to which they give added impetus through their devoted services to Christianity.

[245]

Whoso keepeth his mouth and his tongue keepeth his soul from troubles.

PROVERBS 21:23 *King James Version*

A good name is rather to be chosen than great riches, and loving favour rather than silver and gold.

PROVERBS 22:1 *King James Version*

MRS. WENDELL WILLKIE

THESE TWO PROVERBS, I feel, are good to live by—and the thinking of both was impressed upon me early by my family.

MRS. WENDELL WILLKIE, widow of the Republican Party's choice to oppose the unprecedented third term of President Roosevelt, maintains an apartment in New York City. But she loves to travel and does so, frequently to Europe as well as to various parts of the United States.

Mrs. Willkie, a modest and unassuming woman, is reticent in projecting herself into the limelight. But she becomes animated when she tells of her work for and interest in the American Battle Monuments Commission to which she was appointed by President Eisenhower. She has inspected many of the cemeteries under the Commission's jurisdiction.

During her husband's "crusade to save democracy" in 1940, Mrs. Willkie made the entire campaign swing with the GOP standard bearer. In some industrial cities, her husband was the target of eggs, tomatoes, and others missiles. And on two occasions eggs splashed on Mrs. Willkie.

Neither she nor her husband seemed to be outraged by the incidents, unusual in a Presidential campaign. In fact, Mr. Willkie in one case asked leniency for a schoolboy who had tossed an egg into his car. The boy's training he said was at fault. And Mr. Willkie said those who booed and egged him represented a type of "closed mind" unwilling to consider the real issues.

Mrs. Willkie is concerned too with helping to open the minds and hearts of people to better understanding. She is active in National Conference of Christian and Jews educational programs in behalf of brotherhood, and she serves on the boards of The Salvation Army, the USO, and the New York World's Fair.